AMERICAN IMMIGRATION
QUESTIONS AND ANSWERS

AMERICAN IMMIGRATION
QUESTIONS AND ANSWERS

Olusegun Asekun
New York Licensed Immigration Attorney

Pyxidia House Publishers

AMERICAN IMMIGRATION QUESTIONS AND ANSWERS

Request for information on this title should be addressed to

Olusegun Asekun
The Law Office of Olu Asekun, PC
607 E Abram Street, Suite 9
Arlington, TX 76010 USA
Email: info@olufairdeal.com
+1 817-274-1144. +1 817-274-1844.

Library of Congress Cataloging-in-Publication Data

Olusegun Asekun
AMERICAN IMMIGRATION QUESTIONS AND ANSWERS
ISBN-13: 978-1-946530-12-7 (Paperback)
ISBN-10: 1-946530-12-3 (Paperback)
1. Law - Immigration - Non-fiction 1. Title
Library of Congress Control Number: 2017918126

Published in Dallas Texas by Pyxidia House Publishers. A registered trademark of Pyxidia Concept llc. www.pyxidiahouse.com info@pyxidiahouse.com

Printed in the United States of America

DEDICATION

This book is dedicated to Almighty God, and to the founding fathers of the United States of America, whose vision gave people like me the opportunity to achieve the American dream.

APPRECIATION

I wish to express my profound gratitude to my family, nuclear and extended, as well as my office family.

LEGAL DISCLAIMER

Every single case is unique. This book is not a substitute for legal advice. It is not intended as one cap fits all. It is important to note that two cases with similar facts may end up with completely different outcome. Immigration law is complex.

Readers are advised to consult an experienced immigration attorney for advice on specific cases.

TABLE OF CONTENTS

INTRODUCTION

Merriam-Webster dictionary define knowledge as "the sum of what is known: the body of truth, information, and principles acquired by humankind". Ignorance on the other hand is lack of knowledge or information. Knowledge is an important part of daily life. While not discounting the power and the will of the Almighty God, the difference between success and failure is knowledge.

As an experienced immigration Attorney, I receive immigration questions on daily basis from clients from different parts of the world, including Europe, Middle East, South America, Asia, Africa, Australia, and North America (Canada and the United States). I usually spend about twenty (20) hours per week answering these questions.

This job exposed me to the unexpected level of ignorance common among most people desiring to live in the United States. There are many people who are better off living in their home country rather than coming to the United States. Ignorance has led some people to spend the better part of their adult life living under voluntary bondage in the United States. A journey that could have been undertaken in fifteen days have caused some people fifteen years without reaching their destination. Every time I thought I had seen it all, I am immediately exposed to another ignoramus. Therefore, I decided to educate as many people as I can possibly educate. I have organized pro bono seminars in different communities on the way American immigration system works.

Having done this for more than a dozen years, it became a burden for me to document some of the most common questions I get regularly as well as the answers. The motive of this book is therefore to help as many people as possible to understand the way immigration law works in the United States. If this book is able to help at least one person make the right decision, or help at least one person correctly navigate the American immigration system, my dream would have been fulfilled. With that in mind, enjoy the reading.

Olusegun Asekun,
February 2018

PART ONE

NON-IMMIGRANT VISA QUESTIONS

NON-IMMIGRANT VISA

Question 1:

What is a non-immigrant visa and how is it different from immigrant visa?

Answer:

A non-immigrant visa is a temporary visa that requires a foreign national coming to the US to return to his or her home country on completion of the purpose for which he or she temporarily visited the United States.

Examples of non-immigrant visas are:

B1: Foreign national coming to the United States as a visitor for pleasure

B2: Foreign national coming to the United States as a visitor for business

E: Foreign national coming to the United States under and in pursuance of the provisions of a treaty of commerce and navigation between the United States and the foreign country, of which the alien is a citizen or national

F-1: Foreign national coming to the United States to pursue a full time academic course of study at an accredited institution in the United States.

G: Employee of International organizations.

H-1B: Temporary skilled foreign workers with a minimum of bachelor's degree.

H-2B: Foreign national coming temporarily to the United States to perform agricultural labor or services on a seasonal basis. (Usually for a period of ten months).

H-3: Foreign national coming temporarily to receive training from a U.S. employer in any field other than graduate education.

J: Foreign national who have no intention of abandoning his/her residence in a foreign country coming temporarily to the United States as a participant in a program designated by the Director of the United States Information Agency, for the purpose of teaching, instructing or lecturing, studying, observing, conducting research, consulting, demonstrating special skills or receiving training and who, if coming to the United States to participate in a program under which he will receive graduate medical education or training.

L: Intra-company transferee. It is designed to permit the transfer of foreign national working for a foreign company to the United States to continue working for the same foreign company, its subsidiary, branch, parent, or affiliate in the United States on a temporary basis. It is available for managers or executives (L-1A) and foreign employees with specialized knowledge (L-1B)

M-1: Foreign national coming to the United States to

pursue a full time non-academic course of study (Vocational Students) at an accredited institution in the United States

O: Available for foreign individuals with extra-ordinary ability in the sciences, arts, education, business, or athletics, or foreign nationals with proven record of extraordinary achievement in the film/movie industry and has been recognized locally (nationally) or internationally for their work.

P: Available for foreign nationals who is an athlete or a member of an athletic team; entertainer or a member of an entertainment group; performer or a member of a performing group who is recognized internationally as an individual or a part of an internationally recognized team or group.

Q: Available for foreign nationals coming to the United States to participate in an established international cultural exchange program for the purpose of providing practical training and employment and to share the history, culture, and traditions of home country with the United States.

R-1: Available for foreign nationals coming temporarily to the United States SOLELY to perform services as a minister or services in other religious occupation.

T: Available for, and allow foreign nationals who are victims of human trafficking to remain and work temporarily in the United States to assist in the investigation, and/or prosecution of human trafficking.

U: Available for victims of certain criminal activity who have suffered mental or physical abuse and are helpful to law enforcement or government officials in the investigation and, or prosecution of criminal activity.

V: Available for Non-immigrant Spouse and children of permanent resident with a pending Petition for Alien Relative, Form I-130, filed on or before December 21, 2000.

Immigrant visas:

Immigrant visa on the other hand, are petitions or applications that leads to permanent residency in the United States. Examples are:

K-1: Fiancée of a United States citizen going to marry and stay in the United States

K-3: Spouse of a United States citizen awaiting approval of relative petition

IR1 and CR1: Immediate relative and conditional relative of a United States citizen.

I-140: Immigrant petition for alien worker

I-360: Immigrant petition for religious worker

I-526: Immigrant petition for alien entrepreneur

DV: Diversity visa lottery winners

Asylum application may also be considered an immigrant application. This is because an applicant may use an approved asylum as the basis for applying for legal permanent resident in the United States one (1) year after the grant of Asylum, provided the applicant is still qualified as an Asylee or as the spouse or child of a refugee.

B1/B2 (VISITOR)'S QUESTIONS

Question 2:

I applied for a tourist visa and the embassy denied my application, what can I do?

Answer:

Non-immigrant visas are discretionary. Applicants are generally required to demonstrate family, employment, and financial ties to their home country to establish that it is more likely than not that an applicant will return to his or her home coutry at the end of the period authorized.

Although the United States Department of State establishes some basic criteria to meet these requirements, it is the subjective examination of the applicant by the consular officer that ultimately determines whether a visa application is approved or not.

Where a non-immigrant visa application is denied, the applicant cannot appeal or do anything about it except to re-apply.

Question 3:

I applied for an immigrant visa and the embassy denied my application, what can I do?

Answer:

Unlike a non-immigrant visa, where an immigrant visa application is denied, the Department of State is required to return the case to United States Citizenship and Immigration Services (UCIS) with a recommendation for additional review and or possible revocation of the initial approval. USCIS must then provide the petitioner an opportunity, usually 30 days, to respond to the adverse information or reason for the intended revocation.

Thereafter, USCIS would evaluate the adverse information and Petitioner's response and then decide whether to revoke or reaffirm the approval. If the petition is revoked, the Petitioner would have an opportunity to appeal either to Board of Immigration Appeals (BIA or the Board) or Administrative Appeals Office (AAO) as the case may be. If on the other hand the petition is reaffirmed, an immigrant visa would be issued to the applicant at the US embassy.

Question 4:

I have a valid unexpired non-immigrant visa. Can I be denied admission into the United States at the point of entry? If yes, why?

Answer:

Yes. A valid unexpired non-immigrant visa does not guarantee admission into the United States. A non-immigrant visa is a document directed to airlines authorizing them to bring the bearer into the United States without violating the law. Non-immigrant visa's role therefore terminates upon the airline landing at the port of entry.

The decision to either admit or deny admission to the bearer at this stage is that of Custom and Border Protection (CBP) officers at the point of entry. The decision at this stage is also discretionary and there is no provision for appeal.

However, where the applicant for admission establish a genuine fear of returning to his or her home country, the applicant will be given a credible fear interview before a decision on his or her case is made. In this case, the CBP officers may either detain the applicant or release him/her to a relative until a decision is made.

Where a credible fear is established, the applicant is then given an opportunity to apply for Asylum at the immigration court. The fact that credible fear is established does not mean that asylum will be granted. The applicant would still be required to establish eligibility for asylum on the basis of race, nationality, religion, membership in a particular social group, and/or political opinion.

The applicant at this stage is handed over to Immigration and Customs Enforcement ("ICE") officers. CBP would decide whether or not to parole the applicant. ICE may also decide whether or not to release the applicant on bond. If ICE officers decided not to release the applicant on bond, the applicant may apply to the immigration court for the review of ICE's decision on bond. However, if the alien is charged in the Notice to Appear (NTA) as an arriving alien, the immigration court would not have jurisdiction to review ICE's decision on bond.

Where the applicant is paroled, he/she may use the I-94 to apply for employment authorization. Such employment authorization document usually expires at the same time as the expiration of the parole. CBP at its discretion may or may not extend the parole while the applicant's case is pending at the immigration court.

CBP policy on parole changes from time to time. However, current policy is that the public interest is served by paroling aliens who arrived in the United States at a point of entry (with or without a visa) and are found to have a credible fear of persecution or torture in their home country.

Safeguards, including monthly reporting to ICE field offices by the alien; establishment of alien's identity; and establishment that the alien poses no flight risk and danger to the community, are put in place before the alien is granted parole.

Question 5:

I have a B1/B2 visa. Can I change my status while in the United States?

Answer:

Most people with B1/B2 visas may be able to change their status while in the United States. However, the change of status application must be filed before the expiration of the authorized period. (Before I-94 expires) Where the applicant was given 6 months to stay in the United

States by CBP officers, the change of status application must be submitted and received by USCIS before the expiration of the 6 months. It is pertinent to note that change of status to some non-immigrant status is very technical and approval is not automatic.

Question 6:

Are all categories of visa eligible for change of status?

Answer:

No. Some visa categories are not eligible for change of status. These categories include:

1. Visa Waiver program

2. Crewman

3. Alien in transit or in transit without a visa

4. Fiancée or spouse of a US citizen or dependent of a fiancée or spouse. This is because a fiancée or spouse of a US citizen is seen as a potential immigrant, and not a non-immigrant. They are therefore eligible for adjustment of status and not change of status.

5. Informant and accompanying family on terrorism or organized crime.

6. Foreign medical graduate on International exchange visitor (J-1) unless the alien receives a special waiver.

Question 7:

I have a B1/B2 visa. I was given 6 months at the point of entry. Can I extend my status while in the United States?

Answer:

Yes. You can extend your status. The applicant must explain the reason why extension is required. The applicant must also provide documentary evidence of how he or she intends to take care of himself or herself without recourse to public funds. Evidence may include but not limited to; bank statements showing that the applicant has sufficient funds to take care of himself or herself, evidence that the applicant has a job abroad which he or she does not intend abandoning.

The applicant may also provide a sponsor who will need to complete Form I-134 (Affidavit of support for non-immigrants). For this purpose, (unlike I-864 where only United States citizen and legal permanent resident, can sponsor a foreigner), an applicant for an extension of B1/B2 status may be sponsored by a non-resident.

Where the sponsor is a non-resident, only evidence of financial status and intent to sponsor will be required (Notarized letter from the sponsor confirming sponsorship and bank statements).

Question 8:

What is I-94?

Answer:

I-94 is Arrival/Departure record. It used to be a card

given to non-immigrants at the point of entry. However, it is now electronic. The period authorized is only stamped on passports nowadays. A copy of your I-94 may be retrieved from https://i94.cbp.dhs.gov

Question 9:

My passport was not stamped to indicate how long I have been authorized to stay in the US. How can I find out?

Answer:

With your international travel passport, you log in to https://i94.cbp.dhs.gov to find out how long you have been authorized to stay in the United States.

Question 10:

I entered the United States with a B1/B2 visa. I was authorized to stay for 6 months. Can I work?

Answer:

No. You cannot work. Visitors are not allowed to work while on temporary visit to the United States.

Question 11:

My parent was previously deported. I am a US citizen; how can I bring him/her back?

Answer:

Anyone who has been deported from the US is barred from coming back to the US for a period of 10 years. Available waiver may not cover parent in this example. You should contact an experienced immigration

Attorney for advice on how to resolve your specific case.

Question 12:

I have a B1/B2 visa; can I change to Student status while in the United States?

Answer:

Yes, but it is a technical procedure. There are many factors to consider before attempting changing to Student status while in the United States on B1/B2. The change of status application may be denied for several reasons, including but not limited to, declaring a false purpose of entering the United States; the start of the class will be more than 30 days after the expiration of the period of authorized stay in the United States (It is immaterial that the change of status application was submitted and received by USCIS before the expiration of the period of authorized stay); insufficient evidence of financial support; insufficient evidence of intention to return to home country at the end of the authorized stay period.

It is advisable that an applicant for change of status from B1/B2 also apply for an extension of the B1/B2 while the change of status application is pending and before the expiration of the I-94. It is suggested that an applicant consult an experienced immigration Attorney before embarking on this type of application.

Question 13:

Is change of status from B1/B2 to F-1 guaranteed if you satisfy all the requirements?

Answer:

All non-immigrant status involves element of discretion. For that reason, nothing is guaranteed. However, there are guidelines to prevent abuse of discretion. All things being equal, if all the requirements are met, it is more likely than not that the change of status application would be approved.

Question 14:

I have a 2-year B1/B2 visa. I was given 6 months at the point of entry. My 6 months has expired but my visa is still valid. Can I change my status in the U.S.? If not, can I go out of the U.S. and come back with my visa?

Answer:

No. Your visa does not determine your legal status in the United States. The number of weeks or months given to you at the point of entry determines your legal status. In addition, once your legal status expires, you become an overstayed alien. Going out of the United States at this time may subject you to 3 and 10-year bar depending on how long you overstayed.

If you overstayed for a period of more than 6 months but less than 12 months, and then leave the United States, you will be barred from entering the United States for 3 years. If you overstayed for a period of 1 year or above, and then leave the United States, you will be barred from entering the United States for 10 years. This is known as the 3 and 10-year bar.

Question 15:

If you are in the US on a visiting visa and you apply for a 6 (six) months extension of your B1/B2 status and it was denied, what happens next?

Answer:

If your initial I-94 has expired, it simply means that you are out of status, but if your initial I-94 is still current, you may either depart the United States immediately or apply for a change of status to another non-immigrant status. In this specific scenario, F-1 (student status) may not be approved because most of the time, change of status to F-1 requires that you extend your initial I-94, and because the extension request has already been denied, it is more likely than not that you will be out of status before your F-1 application is adjudicated.

Question 16:

I am on B1/B2 visitor status. I was granted 6-months on my I-94. I applied for, and was granted a 6-month extension of my I-94. Can I apply for another 6 months extension?

Answer:

Visiting status is usually not granted beyond 1 (one) year. If you were initially granted 6 months at the point of entry, and it was extended for another 6 months, you would have been on visiting status for 1 (one) full year and it may not be extended except for overwhelming humanitarian reason.

F-1 (STUDENT) STATUS QUESTION

Question 17:

I am on a student status. Can I change my school?

Answer:

Yes. You may be able to change your school. Your new school must be ICE accredited and be able to issue a new I-20. Your old school must transfer your I-20 to the new school. You may not start with the new school until your I-20 has been transferred from your old school, and received by both ICE and your new school.

Question 18:

I applied for a change of status to F-1 (student status). My application is still pending but my class is about to start, can I resume class while application is pending?

Answer:

No. You have to wait until your student status is approved. If you resume class before approval, it is a violation of your status and your application would be denied.

Question 19:

I am on F-1 (Student status). Can I work?

Answer:
You can only work on campus for up to 20 hours per week. Students cannot work outside campus and cannot work full time on campus without violating the terms of F-1.

Question 20:
I was on F-1 (Student status). I have been out of school for a year. How can I go back to student status?

Answer:
You will need to apply for reinstatement of status. You will have to obtain a new Form I-20, provide evidence of how you intend to pay your school fees and expenses, provide an explanation of why you stopped going to school in the first place, provide evidence that you have not otherwise violated your status, which means that you have to provide evidence that you were not working illegally, you have not falsely represented yourself to be a US citizen. Example of a valid explanation is if you stopped going to school because of health reason.

Question 21:
I am on F-1 (student status) and my spouse is on F-2. Can my spouse work or go to school?

Answer:
No. Your spouse cannot work or go to school. For your spouse to work he or she will need employment authorization Document (EAD) and for your spouse to go to school, he or she would have to change

to F-1. However, minor children may go to school.

Question 22:

I am on A status (Diplomatic and other government officials and their families and employees). Is my spouse required to change status before he/she can go to school?

Answer:

No. The spouse of someone on A status can go to school without changing their status for as long as the principal maintains the original non-immigrant status.

Question 23:

What other non-immigrant status allows a spouse to go to school without applying for change of status to F-1 student status

Answer:

If you are in the United States as the spouse or child of someone in any of the following non-immigrant visa categories, and you wish to attend school in the United States, you do not need to change your status to F-1 student status before you can go to school for as long as your spouse or parent maintains their original non-immigrant status:

1. **E status.** (International Trade and Investors).

2. **G status** (Representatives to International organizations and their families and employees).

3. **H status** (Non-immigrant temporary workers)

4. **R status** (Temporary Religious workers)

5. **I status** (Representatives of foreign media and their families)

6. **J status** (Exchange Visitor and their families)

7. **L status** (Intra-company Transferees)

Question 24:

I am on F-1 status. Is my spouse required to change to F-1 in order to attend elementary, middle, or High school?

Answer:

If you are in the United States as the spouse or child of someone in the F (Academic Student) or M (vocational Student) visa category, you are not required to change your status if you wish to attend elementary, middle, or high school in the United States.

Question 25:

I am on F-1. I am having serious financial difficulty because my sponsor died. Is there anything I can I do to be able to work while still in school?

Answer:

Yes, you can apply for Employment Authorization Document (EAD) based on severe economic hardship. You will need to provide acceptable evidence of your severe financial difficulty.

Question 26:

What are the available ways someone on F-1 (student status) can work?

Answer:

Available ways are:

1. On campus employment (maximum 20 hours per week). Employment authorization is not required.

2. Optional Practical Training (OPT). It provides an opportunity for students to obtain practical training experience of the student's major area of study.

3. Curricular Practical Training (CPT). It is an alternative work/study program that is offered by sponsoring employers through cooperative agreements with the school. It must be an integral part of an established curriculum.

4. Science, Technology, Engineering, or Mathematics (STEM OPT). Students that obtained a degree in any of these fields from an accredited SEVIS certified school may apply for an extension of their OPT. The student can only work for an employer that is enrolled and is in good standing with E-Verify.

5. Cap Gap OPT. Students who have a prospective employer apply for H-1B status on their behalf (whether pending or approved) may apply for Cap Gap OPT to enable them remain and continue to work in the US while waiting for the commencement of the H-1B period.

6. Students may also apply for Employment Authorization Document (EAD) based on any employment that is sponsored by an international organization.

Question 27:

What are the requirements I have to meet to qualify for OPT?

Answer:

In order to qualify for OPT, you must meet the following requirements:

1. You must be in valid F-1 status at the time of your application.

2. You must have completed a program with a minimum of one full academic year.

3. You must be physically present in the United States

4. You must not have been granted OPT previously at the same educational level. In other words, if you were previously granted OPT upon completion of a Bachelor Degree in Accounting, you may not be granted another OPT upon completion of a Bachelor Degree in Computer Science. You may only be granted OPT upon completion of a graduate degree.

Question 28:

I was granted OPT but I have not been able to find a job in the last 3 months. What should I do?

Answer:

If you are granted OPT and you are unable to find a job within 3 months, you must change your status from F-1 to another non-immigrant status or depart the United States.

Question 29:

I have a B1/B2 visa; can I change my status from my home country?

Answer:

No. You can only change your status while already in the United States. However, you can apply for a different non-immigrant status while still in your home country. For example, if you have a valid B1/B2 visa, and you have Form I-20 you can apply for F-1 (Student) status from your home country.

Question 30:

I have a B1/B2 valid visa. I applied for student visa in my home country and was denied. Can I still use my B1/B2 visa?

Answer:

Yes, for as long as your B1/B2 visa was not cancelled.

Question 31:

I have a B1/B2 valid visa. I applied for student visa in my home country and was denied. Can I enter the United States with my B1/B2 and then change to F-1?

Answer:

Yes, but you must be careful to avoid misrepresentation. You may have told the CBP officers at the point of entry that you are coming to the United States temporarily to visit. If you then immediately apply for a change of status to F-1, you may be accused of misrepresenting the purpose of your entry into the United States. If you desire to do this, it is better to consult an experienced immigration Attorney.

H-1B QUESTIONS

Question 32:

How can I obtain a work visa to come to the United States?

Answer:

If you have a degree in a specialty occupation, you may be eligible for work visa (H-1B) visa. Specialty occupations are occupations that require a minimum of four years specialized training culminating in the award of Bachelor Degree. Unless the Degree was obtained in the United States, your credentials must be evaluated and found to be equivalent to a Bachelor Degree awarded by an accredited institution in the United States.

This type of non-immigrant visa requires a United States employer to sponsor a petition on behalf of the applicant. In addition, the applicant's field of study must be relevant to the employer's business. In order words, a Law Office cannot submit a petition to hire a Doctor. Such a petition would be denied. H-1B is also a category with annual numerical limit. Applicant who obtained a Master's Degree from an American University has an added advantage.

Question 33:

I am on H-1B status, which has expired. My employer filed a petition for the extension of my H-1B status. Is it okay to continue to work for the employer while waiting for the approval of the petition to extend my status?

Answer:

Yes. You can continue to work for up to 240 days (Ten months) while waiting for the approval of the petition to extend your H-1B status. The authority for this position is 8 CFR 274a.12(b)(20).

8 CFR 274a.12(b)(20)

"(20) A nonimmigrant alien within the class of aliens described in paragraphs (b)(2), (b)(5), (b)(8), (b)(9), (b)(10), (b)(11), (b)(12), (b)(13), (b)(14), (b)(16), and (b)(19) of this section whose status has expired but who has filed a timely application for an extension of such stay pursuant to §§ 214.2 or 214.6 of this chapter. These aliens are authorized to continue employment with the same employer for a period not to exceed 240 days beginning on the date of the expiration of the authorized period of stay. Such authorization shall be subject to any conditions and limitations noted on the initial authorization. However, if the district director or service center director adjudicates the application prior to the expiration of this 240 day period and denies the application for extension of stay, the employment authorization under this paragraph shall automatically terminate upon notification of the denial decision"

Question 34:

I am currently on H-1B with an employer. I have a new employer who has submitted a petition to transfer my H-1B. Is it okay to start working for the new employer before the petition to transfer is approved?

Answer:

Yes. You can start working for the new employer as soon as the petition to transfer your H-1B to the new employer has been filed. However, if your current employer is cap exempt and your new employer is subject cap, you may not start the new employment until the commencement of the fiscal year to which your employer is subject to.

Question 35:

I have been on H-1B for six years. My employer has submitted a labor Certification on my behalf but we are still waiting for approval. How can I keep myself in status?

Answer:

You may be able to continue to extend your H-1B status beyond six years if you meet the following conditions:

1. The application for labor certification was filed with the department of labor and has been pending for at least 365 days prior to the date you would have exhausted six years on your H-1B status or

2. The I-140 Immigrant Petition for Alien Worker filed with the USCIS has been pending for at least 365 days prior to the date you would have exhausted six years on your H-1B status and

3. The H-1B extension petition is otherwise approvable

Question 36:

Would I be able to get an extension of my H-1B beyond the 6 years if visa is not available in my category?

Answer:

Yes. Visa availability is not a condition for an extension of H-1B status beyond the 6 initial years. Also, per country visa limitation does not affect it.

Question 37:

How long is an approved labor certification valid after approval?

Answer:

Every approved labor certification comes with annotation of the expiration. The average validity of approved labor certification is 180 days. An approved labor certification must be filed with USCIS within the validity period.

Question 38:

Can an approved labor certification be revoked?

Answer:

Yes. The department of labor may revoke an approved labor certification if a subsequent finding is made that the certification was not justified in the first place. A notice would be given to the employer and the employer would have 30 days to respond to the notice before a final decision is taken. Upon revocation, the employer would also have an opportunity to appeal the decision.

RELIGIOUS STATUS QUESTIONS

Question 39:

I am a Pastor and I have been invited to the US to minister, can I use my B1/B2 to minister while in the US?

Answer:

No. If you are coming to the United States to minister, you will need to apply for R-1 visa.

Question 40:

I am a Pastor in my country. Can I get work permit to work in the United States?

Answer:

If your religious organization is registered in the United States as a non-profit religious organization with 501(c)(3) (Tax Exempt) status, and the religious organization is willing to employ you, the religious organization may submit a petition on your behalf to USCIS. If the petition is approved, you will then apply for R-1 visa to enter the United States to work "SOLELY" for the petitioning religious organization.

Question 41:

Can I set up my own church and use it to petition for myself?

Answer:
No. Religious worker petition is not meant to be a self-petitioning benefit.

Question 42:
I am on R-1 but the religious organization is not paying me the amount stated in the petition. Will that pose a problem?

Answer:
Yes. USCIS frowns at bogus, misleading statements, or misrepresentation in a petition. Petitioners may not pay anything less than the amount and, or benefit stated in the petition. This may lead to revocation, denial of extension petition, and more importantly prevent the beneficiary from becoming a legal permanent resident through the religious status benefit process. There is no problem where the payment is more than the amount stated in the petition.

Question 43:
I am on R-1 and my spouse is on R-2. Can my spouse work?

Answer:
No. Someone on R-2 cannot work.

Question 44:
I am on R-1, and my wife and children are on R-2. Do they need to change to F-1 before they can go to school?

Answer:
No. Someone on R-2 can go to school without changing to F-1. They also do not have to pay international student's rate. They would be admitted as local students.

Question 45
What are the requirements of obtaining R-1 status?

Answer
There are two sets of requirements for R-1. One is on the part of the petitioning religious organization and the other is on the part of the beneficiary.

Petitioning church:

1. Must be a religious organization registered in the United States

2. Must be granted Tax Exempt status by the Internal Revenue Service (IRS)

3. Must have a valid place of worship

4. Must have a valid need for the job position

5. Must have documentary evidence of ability to pay the salary offered. USCIS conducts site inspection of the religious organization and verify information contained in a petition.

Beneficiary:

1. Must have been a member of the religious organization for at least 2 years before the petition is filed

2. There must be documentary evidence of the membership

3. There must also be documentary evidence of beneficiary's credentials

Question 46

How much does a religious organization need to have in its account before petitioning for a religious worker?

Answer:

The religious organization must have enough money to pay all its bills; mortgage or rent, utility bills, telephone bills, salary for current employees; and then have enough left to pay the proffered salary of the beneficiary

Question 47:

How is a proffered salary determined for a religious worker?

Answer:

The salary is determined based on minimum wage and the beneficiary's family size. A religious worker petitioner is not required to contact the Department of labor to determine prevailing wage as with secular employment (H-1B and 140) where the employer must first contact the department of labor and obtain prevailing wage before a petition could be filed with USCIS. However, the petitioner must show that the beneficiary would not become a public charge.

Question 48:

I am a pastor who came for vacation in the US with B1/B2 visa. While in the United States, I was invited to minister. I was then given honorarium. What should I do?

Answer:

Ministering is considered working in the US. You need R-1 visa in order to work. However, in the above example, the proper thing to do is to report your honorarium by filing Form 1040NR with the Internal Revenue Service (IRS). This does not mean that you have to pay Taxes to IRS, as you may also be able to deduct your expenses, including the cost of your flight ticket to the US. However, you may have violated the conditions of your visiting visa which does not permit a visitor to the United States to work.

Question 49:

I have been on R-1 for 2 years, when can I apply for Green Card?

Answer:

Before you can apply for Green Card based on your R-1 status, your employer will need to file Form I-360 on your behalf. It is only upon approval of Form I-360 that you can apply for Green Card. In order to file the I-360 petition, you will have to show that you have been on full time employment for at least 2-years immediately preceding the date of your petition. You will have to show 2-year pay slips, 2-year W-2s, and 2-year Tax Returns. Your employer will also have to show evidence of continued ability to pay your salary.

Question 50

Can Form I-360 and Green card application be filed concurrently?

Answer:

Form I-360 based on religious ground cannot be filed concurrently with Green Card application. Form I-360 would have to be filed and approved before Green Card application could be filed.

Question 51:

I have been a full-time pastor for 10 (ten) years. My religious organization wants to apply on my behalf. Should we apply for R-1 or Green Card directly?

Answer:

If you have verifiable documentary evidence of your full-time employment and payment for 2 (two) years with the same employer or same religious denomination immediately preceding the filing of your petition, you may be eligible for I-360, otherwise it is better to start with R-1. Verifiable evidence includes 2-year pay slips; 2-year Tax Return; evidence of ministration (program flyers, weekly bulletin); Credentials, certificate of ordination, Degree or Diploma programs or similar evidence that meets the denomination's ordination.

Question 52:

What is the difference between the requirements of R-1 and I-360?

Answer:

Both of them require that the applicant be a member of the petitioning religious organization for a minimum of 2 (two) years immediately preceding the filing of the petition; that the petitioner be qualified as a religious worker (job duties must be religious duties and beneficiary must be ordained where the duty requires ordination); that the petitioner be qualified as a religious organization that is Tax exempt pursuant to Section 501(c)(3) of the internal revenue code. In both cases, Petitioner must show evidence of ability to pay the salary offered.

Question 53

What is the difference between R-1 and H-1B?

Answer

R-1 is meant for applicants who are engaged in religious duties on full time basis while H-1B is meant for secular employment. Only Religious organizations in the United States that are Tax Exempt can file R-1 on behalf of applicants. Any employer may file H-1B petition on behalf of a beneficiary for as long as what the beneficiary studied is relevant to the employer's business. In order words, a Law Office cannot sponsor a petition for a medical doctor.

Question 54

I am currently on OPT with a church. Can the church file a petition on my behalf?

Answer

The church may be able to file a petition on your behalf only if you are able to establish 2-year membership. A major requirement of R-1 is that the applicant must show evidence that he/she has been a member of the religious organization for at least 2 years prior to the date of petition.

Question 55

My religious organization wanted to file a petition on my behalf but they do not have the money to pay my salary. What can we do?

Answer

The religious organization may use other forms of compensation apart from cash. Example, the religious organization may provide accommodation, transportation, feeding etc., as a form of compensation in lieu of cash. However, whatever form of payment the church intended to use must be properly documented. For example, if the church intends to give you accommodation as part of your remuneration, the petition must include lease agreement or other evidence of ownership or lease of clergy housing. The cover letter must also clearly indicate the intention to include housing as additional compensation.

Question 56

My R-1 has expired but my employer submitted a petition for extension before the current one expired. Is it okay to continue to work for the employer before the petition for extension is approved?

Answer

Yes. You can continue to work for up to 240 days (Ten months) while waiting for the petition to extend your R-1 to be approved. The authority for this position is 8 CFR 274a.12(b)(20)

Question 57

I have been on R-1 for two years. My employer has submitted a Form I-360 on my behalf and it is currently pending. Can I continue to work for the employer and does that keep me in legal status?

Answer

No. The fact that a Form I-360 is currently pending on your behalf does not keep you in status and it does not authorize you to continue to work for the employer. In order to maintain legal status and to legally continue to work for the employer, the religious organization (the petitioner) will need to apply for an extension of your current R-1 status.

Please note that the maximum time you may stay on R-1 at a stretch is five years. Therefore, your employer may only be able to apply for the extension of the R-1 only if you have been on R-1 for less than five years.

Question 58

What is the maximum number of people a church can petition for?

Answer

There is no specific number. It depends on the religious

organization's legitimate needs and financial capacity to pay both existing and new employees in addition to other bills.

During physical inspection, the petitioner would need to explain the circumstances that created the need for beneficiary job position. The religious organization would also have to provide documentary evidence of how it intends to compensate the beneficiary in addition to other financial commitments.

J-1 STATUS QUESTIONS

Question 59:

Can someone on J-1 status change status in the US?

Answer:

No. J-1 status holders are required to return to their home country for two years upon completion of their program. However, a J-1 visa holder may request a waiver of the two-year foreign residency requirement in some cases. If the wavier is granted, the applicant will be able to change his or her status or apply for adjustment of status.

Question 60:

On what grounds can someone apply for a waiver of J-1 two-year foreign residency requirement?

Answer:

An application for a waiver of J-1 two-year foreign residency requirement may be made on any of the following 5 (five) grounds:

1. No objection statement from applicant's home country. Foreign medical physicians who acquired J-1 status on or after January 10, 1977, for the purpose of receiving graduate medical education or training cannot use this option.

2. Request by an interested US Federal Government

Agency. This request may be made by the federal agency if the agency determines that your departure for two years would be detrimental to its interest. An interested federal agency may also make this request on behalf of foreign physicians who agree to serve in health professional shortage areas or medically underserved areas.

3. If an applicant believes that he/she would be persecuted on the basis of race, religion, nationality, membership in a particular social group, or political opinion.

4. Exceptional hardship to a U.S. citizen or lawful permanent resident spouse or child of an exchange visitor.

5. Conrad State 30 Program. This means that a designated State Public Health Department or its equivalent may request the waiver on behalf of a foreign medical graduate who meet the following conditions:

a. Applicant must have an offer of full time employment at a health care professional shortage area or at a health care facility that serves patients from such a designated area.

b. Applicant must agree to begin employment at that facility within 90 (ninety) days of receiving a waiver

c. Applicant must sign a contract to work full time (minimum of 40 hours per week) for a minimum of 3 (three) years after receiving the waiver.

Question 61:

I came with a J-1 visa as a research scholar. My visa has the 2-year foreign residence requirement. Is it possible to change my status while in the US?

Answer

No, except you meet the requirements of a waiver

Question 62

Can a foreign medical graduate on J-1 Status obtain a waiver to change his/her status in the US?

Answer

No, except the applicant obtained a waiver ONLY under Conrad State 30 program. Where a foreign medical graduate obtained a hardship waiver or persecution waiver, the applicant may still not be able to change or adjust status. (See INA 248(a)(2) and 8 CFR 248.2)

Question 63

How can a foreign medical graduate who obtained a J-1 hardship or persecution waiver benefit from the waiver?

Answer

Foreign medical graduate may benefit from a J-1 hardship or persecution waiver only by Consular processing, and not by change or adjustment of status. A change or adjustment of status means that the applicant is able to remain in the United States during the processing. Consular processing on the other hand means that the applicant has to depart the United States and do the processing through a U.S. embassy.

TPS QUESTIONS

Question 64:
What is TPS?

Answer:
Temporary Protected Status (TPS) is a temporary immigration status granted to eligible nationals of designated countries (or parts thereof) who are in the United States and are temporarily unable to return to their homeland because of ongoing-armed conflict, environmental disasters, or other extraordinary and temporary conditions.

Question 65:
Is an applicant for TPS required to depart the United States in order to apply?

Answer:
No. TPS beneficiaries are not required to leave the United States.

Question 66:
Can a TPS applicant apply for employment authorization?

Answer:
Yes, a TPS applicant may obtain work authorization.

Question 67:

Does TPS lead to Permanent Resident?

Answer:

TPS does not lead to permanent resident status. However, you may adjust your status to legal permanent resident from TPS status if you meet the other eligibility requirements.

Question 68:

I was granted TPS (Temporary Protected Status). The TPS is about to expire. Can I change my status from TPS?

Answer:

Yes. Although a TPS is an executive action, you can change your status from TPS to any other non-immigrant status. You may also adjust your status from TPS to legal permanent resident (LPR) for as long as you meet other eligibility requirements.

Question 69:

What happens when TPS designation is terminated?

Answer:

When the Attorney General terminates a country's TPS designation, beneficiaries return to the same immigration status they maintained before TPS (unless that status had since expired or been terminated) or to any other status they may have acquired while registered for TPS.

Accordingly, if an alien had unlawful status prior to receiving TPS and did not obtain any status during the TPS period, he or she will revert to that unlawful status upon the termination of that TPS designation.

Question 70

What are the eligibility requirements for TPS?

Answer

An alien who is a national of a country (or alien having no nationality who last habitually resided in that country) designated by the Attorney General is eligible to apply for benefits under the TPS program if he or she establishes continuous physical presence and continuous residence in the United States for a specified period of time; is not subject to several criminal and security-related bars; and timely registers for TPS benefits.

Question 71

Do we have to re-register if the TPS is extended?

Answer

If the Attorney General extends a TPS designation beyond the initial designation period, the beneficiary must timely re-register to maintain his or her benefits under the TPS program.

Question 72

Can I apply for TPS, if I entered the United States after TPS designation has been made for my country?

Answer

Yes, if you are within the registration or re-registration period.

U-VISA QUESTIONS

Question 73:
What is U-visa?

Answer:
A U-visa is a non-immigrant status specifically set aside for foreigners who have suffered substantial mental or physical abuse due to a criminal activity that occurred in the United states or violated the US law.

Question 74:
How long is a U-visa valid?

Answer:
It is valid for four years but may be extended only if the request for extension is based on exceptional circumstances; or extension is required because of delay in consular processing; or the extension is based on a request from law enforcement officers. It is also automatically extended when your Green Card application is pending.

Question 75:
Does U-visa lead to Green Card?

Answer:
Yes, if certain conditions are met

Question 76:
What are the requirements of U-visa?

Answer:
You may be eligible for U-visa if you meet the following requirements:

1. You must have been a victim of certain criminal activities

2. The crime occurred in the United States or is a violation of US law.

3. You must have suffered substantial mental or physical abuse due to the criminal activity.

4. You possess information concerning that criminal activity.

5. Law enforcement authorities must certify that you were helpful, are helpful, or are likely to be helpful in the investigation or prosecution of the criminal activity.

Question 77:
What are the examples of criminal activities that would qualify someone for U-visa?

Answer:
The list of qualifying criminal activities is not exhaustive. Qualifying criminal activities also includes attempt, conspiracy or solicitation to commit any of the offenses. It also includes crimes with similar elements.

Examples of criminal activities that would qualify an alien for U-visa are the following:

1. Rape

2. Sexual Assault

3. Sexual Exploitation

4. Abusive Sexual Contact

5. Incest

6. Prostitution

7. Slave Trade

8. Involuntary Servitude

9. Peonage (the use of laborers bound in servitude because of debt)

10. Blackmail

11. Abduction

12. Trafficking

13. Kidnapping

14. False Imprisonment

15. Hostage taking

16. Unlawful Criminal Restraint

17. Torture

18. Extortion

19. Felony Assault

20. Murder

21. Manslaughter

22. Domestic Violence

23. Female Genital Mutilation

24. Obstruction of Justice

25. Perjury

26. Witness Tampering

27. Stalking

Question 78:

Would I qualify for U-visa if I entered the United States without a visa?

Answer;

Yes, for as long as you meet other eligibility requirements. You will need to apply for a waiver requesting to be granted advance permission to enter as a non-immigrant using Form I-192, Application for

Advance permission to Enter as a Non-immigrant.

Question 79;

Would I still qualify for U-visa if I was a victim of crime and I met all the other requirements but I left the United States?

Answer:

Yes. You will file your U-visa petition with USCIS and upon approval, you will apply for consular processing.

Question 80:

If I am a victim of crime and I am under 21 years old, who will benefit from my U-visa status?

Answer:

If you are under 21 years old and you are a victim of crime, and you meet other eligibility requirements, then you may petition on behalf of the following family members:

1. Your parents

2. Your spouse if you are married

3. Your children

4. Your brothers and sisters that are under 18 years old.

However, if you are over 21 years old and you are a victim of crime, and you meet other eligibility requirements, then you may only petition on behalf of the following family members:

1. Your spouse if you are married

2. Your children

Question 81:

Do I apply for employment authorization together with my U-visa petition or do I have to wait for the petition to be approved before I apply for employment authorization?

Answer:

No, you do not need to apply for employment authorization. Employment authorization will be issued automatically upon approval of U-visa.

Question 82:

Would my family members (derivatives) also get employment authorization automatically upon the approval of U-visa?

Answer:

No. Family members will need to apply for employment authorization separately. It does not come automatically. Application for employment authorization for family members may be submitted together with the petition or separately after the petition is approved. Employment authorization document would not be issued until the U-visa has been approved.

Question 83;

I am a qualifying family member of a U-visa holder but I am yet to apply for a derivative U-visa. My principal has been granted permanent resident but I have never had U-visa status. Am I still able to apply for my derivative U-visa status?

Answer:

No. Once your principal has been granted Green Card, you will no longer be able to apply for your derivative U-visa status. However, upon satisfaction of other conditions for Green Card, you may still be able to apply for your own Green Card.

Question 84:

I am a qualifying family member of a U-visa holder who has been granted Green Card. I have never been granted a derivative U-visa. What is the procedure for applying for Green Card?

Answer:

You will need to file Form I-929, Petition for Qualifying Family Member of U-1 non-immigrant. Form I-929 is the form used to establish whether your family member is eligible to apply for a Green Card as a result of your U-visa based Green Card. If you are in the United States, you may file this petition together with adjustment application or file it separately. However, if you are outside the United States, you will need to file Form I-929 and then pursue consular processing.

Question 85:

I was a victim of crime but the law enforcement officers refused to certify Form I-918 Supplement B for me. What can I do?

Answer:

You may need to consult an experienced immigration Attorney to evaluate your specific case and advise you accordingly.

P-3 VISA QUESTIONS

Question 86:
I am a promoter. I want to bring a group of artist or entertainers to the United States during summer. What do I need to do?

Answer:
You should file a P-3 petition on behalf of the group.

Question 87:
How long is a P-3 visa valid?

Answer:
It is valid for the time needed to complete the event, activity, or performance. However, it may not exceed one year.

Question 88:
Is it possible to extend P-3 status beyond one year?

Answer:
Yes, it may be extended in increments of one year to enable the beneficiary complete the event, activity or performance.

Question 89:
I am a promoter that brought an artist or entertainer to

the United States on P-3 visa. However, the artist decided to go with another promoter for another concert upon the completion of the tour I organized. Is that allowed?

Answer:

A P-3 visa holder may change employer or promoter. However, the new employer or promoter must file a new petition on behalf of the artist or entertainer requesting to employ or extend the artist or entertainer's stay.

Question 90:

Can a P-3 beneficiary commence employment or performance with a new employer or promoter while a new petition is pending?

Answer:

No. The new petition must be approved before the artist or entertainer can commence employment or performance with the new employer or promoter.

Question 91:

Can an artist or entertainer bring his/her spouse or children along?

Answer:

Yes. A P-3 visa holder may bring his spouse and unmarried children under 21 years old. They will be on P-4 status. However, children 21 years old or married children under 21 years old are not covered under P-4.

Question 92:

Are P-4 visa holders eligible to work?

Answer:

No. P-4 visa holders are not eligible to work. However, they may go to school.

Question 93:

What are the requirements for P-3 visa?

Answer:

For P-3 visa, you must be coming to the United States either individually or as a group for the purpose of developing, interpreting, representing, coaching, or teaching a unique or traditional ethnic, folk, cultural, musical, theatrical, or artistic performance or presentation.

In addition, you must be coming to the United States to participate in a cultural event or events which will further the understanding or development of your art form. The program may be of a commercial or non-commercial nature.

Question 94:

Is there a limit to the number of group members that can accompany an artist or entertainer?

Answer:

No. However, you must be able to justify the inclusion of all members. You will need documentary supporting documents in the form of Affidavits, testimonials or letters from recognized experts attesting to the authenticity of your group. You will also need written consultation from an appropriate labor organization.

DEFERRED ACTION (NON-DACA)

Question 95:

I have a friend in Africa whose 8-year-old son is a US citizen with stage 4 Cancer. My friend came into the United States with a visiting visa to take care of his son. Is there a way to get legal status based on the son's condition?

Answer:

Based on this fact, the parents may be eligible for non-DACA Deferred Action. Other than that, there is really no other way to obtain legal status based on the son's condition. If the parent had been living in the United States for up to 10 years, and does not have criminal record, he may have been eligible for Cancellation of removal for non-permanent residents using the son's medical condition as extreme hardship factor.

Question 96:

What is non-DACA Deferred Action?

Answer:

Deferred Action is an exercise of prosecutorial discretion. It is not an affirmative benefit. It does not confer any immigration status. It does not alter the status of someone who entered the United States without a visa. If granted, it would lead to employment authorization, and would also stop the accrual of unlawful presence during its validity. Employment authorization may be renewed for as long as the Deferred Action is valid.

Question 97:

What are the procedures of non-DACA Deferred Action?

Answer:

A request for non-DACA Deferred Action must follow these procedures:

1. Detailed explanation of why the applicant is requesting non-DACA Deferred Action

2. Copy of Requestor's birth certificate

3. Copy of Requestor's biometrics page of Travel Passport

4. Copy of Requestor's visa page, if applicable

5. Copy of Requestor's I-94, Arrival/Departure Record

6. Completed Form G-325A Biographic Information by Requestor

7. Copy of qualifying relative's birth certificate

8. Copies of qualifying relative's medical Records

9. Letters from caring teams; Doctors, Nurses, etc., if applicable

10. Evidence of community and familial ties

11. Evidence of conditions in Requestor's country of origin

Question 98:
Where should a request for non-DACA Deferred Action be made?

Answer:
The request should be submitted to the USCIS field office with jurisdiction over the requestor's place of residence. However, if the requestor is in removal proceedings, the request should be submitted to Immigration and Customs Enforcement (ICE).

Question 99:
Is employment authorization document submitted along with the request?

Answer:
No. Application for employment authorization should be submitted upon the grant of non-DACA deferred action under 8 CFR 274a.12(c)(14).

Question 100:
Can I appeal the decision if my request is denied?

Answer:
No. It is a discretionary relief. However, a requestor may submit additional evidence to request reconsideration of the determination or submit a new request.

Question 101:

How many years can someone be on non-DACA deferred action?

Answer:

For as long as the deferred action has not been terminated by the Regional Director.

PART TWO

IMMIGRANT QUESTIONS

FAMILY BASED QUESTIONS

Question 102:

Can a Legal Permanent Resident (Green Card holder) file a fiancée visa on behalf of a fiancée?

Answer:

No. Only a United States citizen can file a fiancée petition.

Question 103:

Can a Legal Permanent Resident (Green Card holder) file an immigrant petition for spouse and children?

Answer:

Yes except for married adult children over 21 years old. A Green Card holder can petition for spouse, unmarried children under 21 years old, and unmarried children over 21 years old. A Green Card holder cannot petition for married adult children over 21 years old. Only United States citizen can do that.

Question 104:

Can a Legal Permanent Resident file an immigrant petition for parents?

Answer:

No. Only United States citizen can file an immigrant petition for parents.

Question 105:

Can a Legal Permanent Resident petition for brothers and sisters?

Answer:

No. Only United States citizen can file immigrant petition for brothers and sisters.

Question 106:

If a legal Permanent Resident (Green Card holder) file an immigrant petition for an unmarried adult child over 21 and the petition is approved but the child married before entering the United States, or before obtaining Green Card, if in the United States, what happens to the approved petition?

Answer:

The outcome depends on the status of the Petitioner (parent) on the date of marriage. If on the date of Beneficiary's marriage, the Petitioner is still a Legal Permanent Resident (Green Card holder), the approved petition is terminated by operation of law.

However, if the Petitioner has become a United States citizen on the date of Beneficiary's marriage, the category would automatically change from a Green Card holder petitioning for unmarried adult child over 21 years old to United States citizen petitioning for married adult citizen over 21 years old.

Question 107:

How long can a Legal Permanent Resident (Green Card holder) stay outside the United States?

Answer:

A Legal Permanent Resident (Green Card holder) is not expected to stay outside the United States for 6 months or more. When a Green Card holder stays outside the United States for up to 6 months but less than 1 year, he or she may expect to answer questions about his or her trip but he or she does not lose the Green Card.

In addition, a trip outside the United States of 6 months but less than 1 year would disrupt the physical presence requirement of citizenship. However, if a Green Card holder stays outside the United States for 1 year or more, there is a rebuttable presumption of law that the person abandoned the Green Card.

Question 108:

How can someone overcome the rebuttable presumption of law that someone abandoned his/her Green Card?

Answer:

You can overcome the presumption by showing the following:

1. You did not terminate your employment in the United States

2. You did not obtain employment outside the United States

3. Your immediate family members are present here in the United States

4. You retain full access to your home in the United States

Question 109:

With a Green Card, how long do you have to wait to file for family members?

Answer:

There is no waiting period for a Green Card holder to file an immigrant petition for family members. However, filing and getting a petition approved is different from applying for Green card for family members.

For family of Green card holders, they can only apply for Green Card when immigrant visa becomes available. The date the petition was received by USCIS is the determining factor. It is known as the priority date.

Question 110:

If your Green card is expired, can you apply for citizenship?

Answer:

Yes, you can apply for citizenship with expired Green Card for as long as you meet other eligibility requirements for citizenship.

Question 111:

If you are a Green card holder, can you be deported?

Answer:
Yes, on criminal or fraud grounds. If you obtain your Green Card by fraud or you commit crime, you may be deported. However, as a Green Card holder, you are entitled to due process of the law, which means that you will have the opportunity to apply for eligible relief at the immigration court.

You will also have the opportunity to appeal the immigration judge's decision, if you disagree with it, before you can be deported.

Question 112:
I applied for Green Card for my spouse, the application is still pending but my spouse was convicted of DWI, can he/she still get his Green Card?

Answer:
Yes, assuming that there are no other issues of admissibility, but every case is different. Please consult an experienced immigration Attorney who will look at your specific case.

Question 113:
Can a US citizen file petition for stepchildren?

Answer:
Yes, but only if the marriage that created the step relationship occurred before the child or children turned 18 years old.

Question 114:

If your Green Card application has been pending for 3 years and your US citizen spouse who petitioned for you has now divorced you, what would happen to your pending application?

Answer:

Your Green Card application would be denied. Green Card application based on marriage cannot be approved if the marriage is terminated before the Green Card is approved.

Question 115:

I am married to a US citizen who filed a relative petition on my behalf. The petition has been pending for 2 (two) years and we have been invited for interview for the second time. My spouse has threatened not to attend the interview with me because of a misunderstanding we have. Is there anything I can do to get my Green Card approved if he refused to attend the interview with me?

Answer:

No. There is nothing you can do to get the petition approved. He is the petitioner and the petition cannot be approved in his absence. However, my advice to you is to consult an experienced immigration Attorney who will look into your specific case and determine if there are other options available for you.

Question 116:

I obtained my legal permanent resident status through marriage to a US citizen a year ago. I am divorced from him. I am remarried to a new spouse. Can I petition for my new spouse?

Answer:

If you obtained your legal permanent resident status through marriage to a US citizen, you cannot petition for a new spouse for 2-years from the date of your legal permanent resident status. In addition, a new petition before you become a US citizen may trigger a review of your relationship with your US citizen spouse. USCIS would need to determine that you did not obtain your legal permanent resident status by marriage fraud.

Question 117:

I won the DV visa lottery. I got married after I won, but my spouse previously applied for visa at the embassy where he claimed married in his previous application. We were both denied. What can we do?

Answer:

There is nothing you can do about that. Your only chance to present your case is when you attend an interview at the embassy or at USCIS office. Denial of DV lottery visa cannot be appealed. It is also not eligible for waiver of grounds of inadmissibility.

Question 118:

I entered the US with a B-2 visa. I was given 6 months at the point of entry. My 6 months has expired and I just won the DV lottery. Can I apply for adjustment of status?

Answer:

Your adjustment application would be denied because you are already out of status.

Question 119:

I entered the US with a B-2 visa. I was given 6 months at the point of entry. I won the DV lottery. My legal status will expire in April but visa will not be current until October and by that time, I would have been out of status. What should I do?

Answer:

You may apply for a 6-month extension of your status. You may apply for a change of status to another non-immigrant status (example is student status). What you cannot do is to be out of status before October.

Question 120:

Can a Green Card holder be prevented from entering the United States by executive order by the President?

Answer:

The President does not have the authority to legislate on immigrant visas. Only the Congress can do that. A Green Card holder cannot be summarily deported. However, a Green card holder who has committed a crime may be arrested at the point of entry and put on removal proceedings. He would then have the opportunity to apply for any relief he may be eligible for before the immigration judge.

Question 121:

I have a pending adjustment application. I want to travel outside the United States with Advance Parole Document. Is it safe?

Answer:

Generally, anyone coming to the United States is subject to inspection at the port of entry by Customs and Border Protection (CBP) officers to determine eligibility. This includes legal permanent residents. However, bearing any criminal conviction, or any other major issue of eligibility, traveling with advance parole document is safe.

Question 122:

I am a conditional permanent resident. My spouse has filed for divorce. Is there a way I can extend my Green Card without my spouse?

Answer:

Yes, by applying for a removal of condition based on good faith marriage. You must include substantial evidence of good faith marriage with your application.

Question 123:

My husband brought me to the United States on his granted asylum application. He later divorced me. I applied for adjustment of status, but it was denied. What are my options?

Answer:

Since your asylum is based on your husband's

application, your adjustment of status is also attached to your being married to your husband; therefore, your divorce removed the basis of eligibility for adjustment of status. However, your divorce does not take away your asylum. Whenever you remarry (if you decide to do that), your new spouse can file a family petition on your behalf. Otherwise, you may remain in asylum status.

Question 124:

I came to the United States without a visa 20 years ago. I am married to a United States citizen. We have 3 United States citizen children. I do not have any criminal record. How can I obtain Green Card?

Answer:

This is a 4-stage process.

Stage 1: Your spouse should file Form I-130 Petition for Alien Relative on your behalf

Stage 2: Upon approval of the I-130, you should apply for provisional unlawful presence waiver

Stage 3: Resume processing with the National Visa Center

Stage 4: Attend an immigrant visa interview at the US embassy in your home country

Question 125:

Can I be denied visa at the embassy after the Provisional unlawful presence waiver has been granted?

Answer:

Only if you obtain the waiver by fraud or misrepresentation. For example, if you came to the US without a visa and you have been arrested and deported, and you came back to the US illegally, but in your waiver application, you did not disclose your deportation; your immigrant visa may still be denied at the embassy based on your misrepresentation. The waiver can only waive one illegal entry.

Question 126:

I came to the United States without a visa 20 years ago. I am married to a United States citizen. We have 3 United States citizen children. I do not have any criminal record. Is it possible to obtain Green Card without leaving the US?

Answer

Yes, but only if you come to the attention of ICE, and a Notice to Appear (NTA) is issued to you. In that case, you may be able to apply for Cancellation of Removal for non-permanent Resident.

Question 127:

What are the requirements of Cancellation of removal for non-permanent resident?

Answer:

To be eligible for Cancellation of Removal for non-permanent resident, an alien must meet the following requirements:

1. Applicant must show that he/she has been residing in the US for at least 10 years before the date of Notice to Appear (NTA) was issued.

2. Applicant must demonstrate that his/her removal from the United States would create extreme hardship on his/her United States citizen parent(s), spouse, and minor children.

3. Applicant must show that he is a person of good moral character

4. Applicant must demonstrate that he/she deserves a favorable exercise of discretion by the immigration judge.

Question 128:

I am already a permanent resident but I was convicted of a crime, I am now in removal proceedings; what relief can I apply for?

Answer:

Depending on your peculiar situation and the severity of your crime, you may be eligible for cancellation of removal for permanent resident, and you may also be eligible for re-adjustment. Please consult an experienced immigration Attorney who can look into your specific case before advising you.

Question 129:

What are the requirements of cancellation of removal for permanent resident?

Answer:

To be eligible for cancellation of removal for permanent resident, an applicant must meet the following eligibility requirements:

1. Must have been a legal permanent resident for a minimum of 5 years

2. Must have been living continuously in the United States in any legal status for at least 7 years before the date Notice to Appear (NTA) was issued.

3. Must not have been convicted of aggravated felony.

4. Applicant must demonstrate that he/she deserve a favorable exercise of discretion by the immigration judge

Question 130:

Is there any relief for a permanent resident convicted of aggravated felony?

Answer:

Yes. A permanent resident convicted of aggravated felony may be able to concurrently apply for 212(h) waiver and re-adjustment. Stand-alone 212(h) waiver is not available. Therefore, the applicant must have a current immigrant visa immediately available. This is a very technical area of imigration law. It is advisable to consult an experienced immigration Attorney.

Question 131:

What reliefs are available for an alien in removal

proceedings?

Answer:

If you are in removal proceedings, it is advisable to consult an experienced immigration Attorney to look at your peculiar situation and determine the appropriate relief in your case.

However, summary of available reliefs includes:

1. Cancellation of removal for non-permanent resident;

2. Cancellation of removal for legal permanent resident;

3. Adjustment of status;

4. Asylum, Withholding of Removal, and Relief under Convention Against Torture;

5. Voluntary Departure;

6. Termination of proceedings.

Question 132:

I obtained my Green Card together with my parents when I was 10 years old. I am now 22 years old. I am not married. I was convicted of burglary and I just finished serving a 3-year sentence. I am now in removal proceedings. What are my chances?

Answer:

First and foremost, you will need to determine whether or not you are a US citizen. Since you obtained your Green Card at such a young age, it is important to determine your parent's status.

If either of your parents became a US citizen before your 18th birthday, you are a US citizen and you may be able to request a termination of your proceedings. You will need to provide documentary evidence of your claim to the immigration judge.

Question 133:

I am a US citizen. I have my own biological children. Can I adopt a child under 21 whose stay has expired?

Answer:

For immigration purpose, generally you must have adopted the child before his/her 16th birthday. However, a child may be adopted before his/her 18th birthday where the child is the birth sibling of another child who was adopted by the same parent or parents before the other child's 16th birthday and immigrated through the immediate relative process, or the child is the birth sibling of another child who was adopted by the same parent or parents before the other child's 16th birthday and who immigrated as an orphan based on an adoption by the same parent or parents.

In addition, you must have legal and physical custody of the child for at least 2 (two) years while the child was a minor. However, the custody and residence requirements are waived for abused children.

Question 134:

I am married to a US citizen. My spouse wants to file

a petition on my behalf, but he does not have enough income, what can we do?

Answer:

Your spouse will need to submit Form I-864 on your behalf. In addition, you will need a joint sponsor who will also need to complete Form I-864 on your behalf.

Question 135:

How much is my husband required to make in order to petition for me?

Answer:

You will need to look at Form I-864P and also determine your spouse's adjusted gross income as stated on your spouse's most recent Tax Return.

Question 136:

I have a co-sponsor. He is a US citizen, but he is working outside the US. Can he co-sponsor me?

Answer:

The mere fact that he is working outside the United States would not disqualify him for as long as he meets the eligibility requirements. Affidavit of support is meant to ensure that the beneficiary would not become a public charge. Therefore, he would have to present the most recent Tax Return and W-2.

The fact that a US citizen is working outside the United States does not relieve him/her of the obligation to file yearly income Tax. Therefore, once his current Tax

Return shows that he made enough income to be able to sponsor you, he would be eligible to sponsor you.

Question 137:

My spouse cannot find his/her Tax Return, what should we do?

Answer:

Your spouse should either call IRS to request a copy or go to the local IRS office close to you to request a copy.

Question 138:

My birth Certificate is not in English. Do I submit it like that?

Answer:

Every document that is not in English must be translated into English. This is mandatory. The Translator must also certify that he is eligible to translate the document. Usually, it may be notarized.

Question 139:

My US citizen spouse wants to file a petition on my behalf. What forms do we need to file?

Answer:

If you are in the United States, you will need to file the following forms:

1. Form I-130
2. Form I-130A
3. Form I-131

4. Form I-485
5. Form I-765
6. Form G-325A for both Petitioner and Beneficiary
7. Form I-864

Question 140:

My husband is a legal permanent resident. He has submitted a relative petition on my behalf. How can I obtain a work permit?

Answer:

You are not eligible for work permit based on your husband's petition until visa becomes available and you are able to apply for adjustment of status.

Question 141:

I am married to a US citizen who had been previously convicted of child molestation and placed on 10-year probation. He/She successfully completed his/her probation. Can he/she file a relative petition on my behalf?

Answer:

If your spouse's conviction falls within Adam Walsh's Act, the petition may not be approved. Adam Walsh Act prohibit US citizen and lawful permanent resident aliens who have been convicted of specified offense against a minor under 18 years from filing a family based immigrant petition (Form I-130 Petition for Alien Relative); Forms I-600A or I-600 Petition to classify Orphan) and Form I-129F for Fiancée "K" visa status on behalf of any beneficiary. Specified offense includes:

1. An offense involving kidnapping (unless committed by a parent or guardian)

2. An offense involving false imprisonment (unless committed by a parent or guardian).

3. Solicitation to engage in sexual conduct

4. Use in a sexual performance

5. Solicitation to practice prostitution

6. Video voyeurism (whoever, in the special maritime and territorial jurisdiction of the United States, has the intent to capture an image of a private area of an individual without their consent, and knowingly does so under circumstances in which the individual has a reasonable expectation of privacy)

7. Possession, production or distribution of child pornography.

8. Criminal sexual conduct involving a minor, or the use of the Internet to facilitate or attempt such conduct.

9. Any conduct that is by nature a sex offense against a child.

Question 142:

Can someone challenge USCIS decision to deny a petition on Adam Walsh Act ground?

Answer:

No. The Board of Immigration Appeals ("The BIA" or "The Board") has ruled that this decision is not reviewable. (See Matter of Aceijas-Quiroz, 26 I&N Dec. 294 (BIA 2014)

Question 143:

I have a pending Form I-130 Petition for alien Relative and adjustment application. My United States citizen spouse has been convicted and is now in jail. How would that affect my pending petition and application?

Answer:

Every case is different. However, as an experienced immigration Attorney, I have tried 3 different things in this scenario. Incidentally, all of them worked for my clients. The choice of what option is best for you may depend on how long you and your spouse lived together before his/her incarceration; how much evidence of good faith marriage you have; and the officer handling your case. You may try any of the following:

1. Make an infopass appointment and notify USCIS that your United States citizen petitioner is in jail. This may lead to your interview being put on hold or delayed (Please note that it is not guaranteed because there is no specific law that requires USCIS to wait for the petitioner indefinitely, especially where the sentence is a long one).

2. If you have an Attorney, have your Attorney make an arrangement with the Warden of the facility where your spouse is detained for a telephonic interview.

Then Attorney should request telephonic interview with USCIS on the interview date. You and your Attorney would be physically present at USCIS while the petitioner is contacted telephonically. Before you do this, you must make sure that while you were together before he went to jail, you have substantial evidence *bonafides*. You must also have documentary evidence of your visitations to him/her in jail and be sure that you know yourselves well enough to be interviewed separately to avoid a finding of marriage fraud.

3. If you have substantial evidence of *bonafides*, including visitation records, you may request an Affidavit from the petitioner in jail stating that he/she intends to continue with the petition despite being incarcerated. In this situation, USCIS would take a decision based on the evidence on record instead of waiting for your spouse.

Question 144:

What kind of ailments would disqualify someone from getting a Green Card in the United States?

Answer:

Communicable disease of public health significance. Example is tuberculosis.

However, failure to present documentation of having received vaccinations against vaccine preventable diseases may also disqualify an alien from obtaining Green Card. In addition, serious physical or mental disorder with associated harmful behavior. Drug abuse or drug addiction may also disqualify an alien from obtaining Green Card.

Question 145:

My previous spouse filed a petition on my behalf. That petition was denied on the ground of marriage fraud. I am now remarried to another United States citizen. We recently had a baby. My spouse filed a new petition on my behalf. What is the chances of getting it approved?

Answer:

If the previous petition filed on your behalf was denied based on marriage fraud, or attempted marriage fraud, no new petition may be approved for you. Section 204(c) of the immigration and Nationality Act forbids the approval of another petition after a determination that an alien has entered into, or attempted to enter into a marriage fraud.

Question 146:

I am married to a United States citizen who has submitted an I-130 petition on my behalf. I was served with a final decree of divorce from my country by my ex-spouse terminating our marriage. I recently discovered that the divorce was not valid. How would that affect my pending petition?

Answer:

Your petition may be denied. You cannot be married to more than one person at the same time. That would constitute bigamy. However, depending on your State family law, you may escape the consequence if you file a new divorce here in the United States and the divorce became final before your I-130 petition was filed with USCIS.

For example, in Texas, Chapter 6, Subchapter C, Sec. 6.202 of Texas Family Code will rescue you. Please note that if your petition has been filed before your new divorce became final, your petition may not be approved. You will have to withdraw the current petition and submit a new petition.

Question 147:

What are the differences between a US citizen and a Green Card holder?

Answer:

There are a lot of differences between a US citizen and a legal permanent resident. Some of them are:

1. A US citizen can vote in an election. A Green Card holder cannot do that.

2. A US citizen can contest an election and run for office. A Green Card holder cannot do that.

3. A US citizen may petition for parents. A Green Card holder cannot do that.

4. A US citizen can petition for a fiancée. A Green Card holder cannot do that.

5. A US citizen can petition for married children. A Green Card holder cannot do that.

6. A US citizen can petition for brothers and Sisters. A Green Card holder cannot do that.

7. There are some sensitive jobs that only US citizen can hold. For example, only a US citizen may be employed as an immigration officer.

8. A US citizen may stay outside the United States for unlimited number of days, weeks, or years. A Green Card holder cannot do that.

9. A child born to a US citizen anywhere in the world automatically becomes a US citizen. This is not the case with a Green Card holder

10. A US citizen may not be deported for committing a crime. A Green Card holder may be deported for commission of a crime.

11. A US citizen does not have to wait for visa to become available when petitioning for immediate family members. A Green Card holder does have to wait for visa to become available before a family member can apply for Green Card.

Question 148:

What are the differences between a Green Card and employment authorization document?

Answer:

Green Card is a legal permanent status while employment authorization document is temporary and only valid while your adjustment application is pending.

Question 149:

I am a Green Card holder. I work outside the United States. I was coming back to the US recently and the CBP officer wrote "I-327 advised" on my passport. What does that mean?

Answer:

It means that you have been advised to obtain re-entry permit. A re-entry permit is a US passport like booklet issued to Green Card holders who travels too frequently outside the United States or those Green Card holders who are going to be outside the United States for an extended period of time.

Question 150:

What if I failed to apply for the re-entry permit?

Answer:

You stand the risk of jeopardizing your Green Card.

Question 151:

Can I apply for the re-entry permit while outside the United States?

Answer:

No. The process involves biometrics which can only be done inside the United States. In these days of enhanced immigration scrutiny and enforcement, it is advisable that you submit your application for re-entry permit, provide your biometrics before you travel outside the United States. You should also make sure that your Green Card is current and not expired.

In that case, you should have the Receipt notice available with you for presentation at the port of entry so that the CBP officer will know that you have at least complied with the advice to apply for re-entry permit.

Question 152:

Does applying for the re-entry permit have any implication on my immigration status?

Answer:

Yes. It may affect your eligibility for citizenship. When you apply for re-entry permit, it is an indication that you spent more time outside the United States, therefore you may not meet the physical presence requirement for citizenship.

EMPLOYMENT BASED QUESTIONS

Question 153:

I am a small business owner, how old does my business have to be before my business is able to petition for someone?

Answer:

There is no age requirement. However, your business must have documentary evidence of ability to pay proffered salary in addition to other financial obligations of the business.

Question 154:

I have been on F-1 status for 4 (four) years. I just graduated with a Bachelor of Science in Nursing. I am currently on optional practical training (OPT). What can I do to obtain Green Card?

Answer:

All you have to do is to look for an employer in the medical field, hospitals, Nursing homes, home health care agency, Nursing schools, etc., to sponsor a petition on your behalf under EB 3 category. The good thing about your case is that the employer is not required to obtain permanent labor certification before submitting I-140 petition to USCIS on your behalf.

Question 155:
What is permanent labor certification?

Answer:
Permanent Labor Certification is a requirement mandating US employers seeking to employ certain foreigners who are seeking employment for which qualified US citizen workers are not available, to obtain certification from the Secretary of Labor, stating that there are no US workers available to undertake the employment sought by the foreign worker and that the employment of the foreigner would not adversely affect the wages and working conditions of US workers similarly employed.

The determination of labor availability is made at the location where the foreigner intends to work and at the time of the visa application.

Question 156:
Is there an exception to the requirement of labor certification? If yes, what are the exceptions?

Answer:
Yes. There are few exceptions to the requirements of labor certification. They are Schedule A occupations, EB-1 and EB-2A. Schedule A occupations are Nursing and Physical Therapy. EB-1 is an alien of extra ordinary ability; outstanding professor or researcher, or multinational executive or manager.

EB-2A is an alien of exceptional ability seeking National Interest Waiver

Question 157:

I am currently on H-1B status. How can I obtain Green Card?

Answer:

In order to obtain Green Card, your employer must commence the process of labor certification on your behalf. Upon approval, your employer would then file Form I-140 on your behalf. If immigrant visa is available at the time of filing the I-140 petition, you may be able to concurrently file adjustment application with the petition. If immigrant visa is not available, you will have to wait until visa becomes available before you can submit adjustment application.

Question 158:

My spouse is out of status. Is it advisable to include his/her name in my own application for permanent resident? What is the risk of having my application approved if my spouse is included?

Answer:

Yes, it is not only advisable, but it is required. Not including your spouse's name means that you are providing incorrect information on your application. The application requires your marital status and your spouse information. There is no option to providing the information if you are married.

Besides, you will only be able to help your spouse in the future if he/she is already listed on your application. Your spouse may be out of status today but you may be able to file a family petition to regularize his/her status when you become a US citizen. You risk not being able to do that if his/her name is not listed.

There is no risk in getting your application approved if your spouse is listed. He is only going to be considered in evaluating your background. The only risk here is not including your spouse on your application.

Question 159:

The United States government employed me in my home country. Can that give me a pathway to becoming a legal permanent resident of the United States?

Answer:

Yes. Employees and former employees of the US government abroad may be eligible for EB-4 special immigrant category.

Question 160:

What requirements does foreign employees working for the US government abroad need to meet in order to be eligible to apply for lawful permanent resident under EB-4 category?

Answer:

Current or former employees of the United States abroad, including spouse and children, may be eligible for legal permanent resident through the EB-4 category upon satisfaction of the following:

1. The employee or former employee must have a minimum of individual or combined 15 (Fifteen) years of faithful service.

2. The foreign employee must receive a recommendation from the principal officer of a United States foreign service establishment based on exceptional circumstances.

3. The recommendation must be approved by the State Department Headquarters in Washington DC.

4. If the employee is retired, the retirement must be honorable. In other words, the employee must not have been fired, or resigned when he/she would have been fired.

Question 161:

What category of foreigners are eligible to apply Green Card through the EB-1 category?

Answer:

The following category of foreigners are eligible for Green Card under the EB-1 category:

1. Foreign nationals of extraordinary ability in the sciences, arts, education, business or athletics.

2. Foreign nationals that are outstanding professors or researchers.

3. Foreign nationals that are managers and executives subject to international transfer to the United States.

Question 162:

What category of foreigners are eligible for Green Card under the EB-2 category?

Answer:
The following category of foreigners are eligible for Green Card under the EB-2 category:

1. Foreign nationals of exceptional ability in the sciences, arts or business.

2. Foreign nationals that are advanced degree professionals.

3. Qualified alien physicians who will practice medicine in an area of the United States, which is underserved.

Question 163:
What category of foreigners are eligible for the EB-3 category?

Answer:
The following category of foreigners are eligible for Green Card under the EB-3 category:

1. Foreign national professionals with bachelor's degrees (not qualifying for a higher preference category).

2. Foreign nationals skilled workers (minimum of two years training and experience)

3. Foreign national unskilled workers

Question 164:
What category of foreigners are eligible for the EB-4 category?

Answer:

The following category of foreigners are eligible for Green Card under the EB-4 category:

1. Foreign national religious workers.

2. Employees and former employees of the United States government abroad.

Question 165:

What category of foreigners are eligible for the EB-5 category?

Answer:

Immigrant Investors and family members (spouse and unmarried children under 21) who fall into one or more of the following categories:

*Please note that the amount may change from time to time.

1. Those who have invested or are actively in the process of investing at least $1,000,000 (One Million Dollars) or

2. Those who have invested or are actively in the process of investing at least $500,000 (Five Hundred Thousand Dollars) where the investment is being made in a "targeted employment area" which is an area that has experienced unemployment of at least 150 per cent of the national average rate.

Question 166:

I applied for Green Card based on my approved

Form I-140 Immigrant Petition for Alien Worker and my Form I-485 Application to Register Permanent Resident or adjust Status has been pending for more than six months. Can I change my employer?

Answer:

Yes. You may be able to change your employer if you meet the following requirements:

1. Your application has been pending for more than 180 days.

2. The new employment is the same or similar classification as the one you were doing.

Question 167:

Would I still be able to change my employer if my Form I-140 Immigrant Petition for Alien Worker was concurrently filed with my Form I-485 Application to Register Permanent Resident or Adjust status and both have been pending for more than 180 days?

Answer:

Yes, for as long as the new employment is the same or similar classification as the one you were doing.

Question 168:

Is there a notification requirement to USCIS on change of employer?

Answer:

Yes. The new employer is required to send a letter to

USCIS verifying that the job offer exists and stating the new job title, the new job description and the new salary. The letter should also state that the new employer intend to employ the beneficiary permanently.

Question 169:

Can I change employer if the priority date is not current or do I have to wait until it is current?

Answer:

Yes, you can change employer for as long as the new employment is the same or similar classification as the one you were doing. Priority date does not have to be current for you to do this.

Question 170:

Is it possible to change employer after my adjustment application has been pending for more than 180 days where I have never worked for the petitioning employer?

Answer:

Yes. However, there must be evidence that the job offer is not illusory. It must be shown that there was a genuine intent to employ you permanently at the time the I-140 immigrant petition for alien worker was approved.

Question 171:

Can I change employer where the petitioning employer prior to 180 days withdrew the approved Form I-140 Immigrant petition by alien worker?

Answer:

No. Where the petitioning employer withdrew the petition before 180 days, you cannot change employer because there would be nothing to change as nothing is pending after the withdrawal.

Question 172:

Can I change employer where the petitioning employer after 180 days withdrew the approved Form I-140 Immigrant petition by alien worker?

Answer:

Yes, you may be able to change your employment if the new employment is the same or similar classification as the one you were doing and the new employer met the other conditions.

Question 173:

When there is a change of employer, is the new salary required to be the same as the previous salary?

Answer:

No. The new salary does not have to be exactly the same. However, the new salary cannot be less than the amount indicated in the approved labor certification.

IMMIGRANT INVESTOR QUESTIONS

Question 174:

How do I determine "targeted employment area"?

Answer:

Targeted employment areas are usually upon approval by USCIS designated as regional centers. The regional centers would have passed the test of targeted employment area. In other words, investment through a regional center is an investment in a "targeted employment area".

Question 175:

How can I obtain Green Card as an investor?

Answer:

You will need to invest in the United States either in a regional center or personally. Either way, you must demonstrate that your investment:

1. Will benefit the United States economy and create the requisite number of full time jobs for qualified persons within the United States.

2. Create full time employment for not fewer than 10 qualified individuals.

3. Maintain the number of existing employees at no less than the pre-investment level for a period of at least two years, where the capital investment is being made in a "troubled business", which is a business that has been in existence for at least two years and that has lost 20 percent of its net worth over the past 12 to 24 months.

Investors may establish a new commercial enterprise by creating an original business or purchase an existing business and simultaneously or subsequently restructuring or reorganizing the business such that a new commercial enterprise results, or by expanding an existing business by 140 percent of the pre-investment number of jobs or net worth, or retaining all existing jobs in a troubled business that has lost 20 percent of its net worth over the past 12 to 24 months.

If you decide to invest through a regional center, you will only need to wire your funds and administrative fee to the regional center.

Thereafter, you will submit Form I-526 Immigrant Petition for Alien Entrepreneur to USCIS along with an explanation of the source and path of your funds as well as the supporting documents, including the evidence of wiring.

Upon approval of the Petition, you will be able to apply for adjustment of status (if you are physically present in the United States) or apply for permanent residence through the consulate (if you are outside the United States).

Question 176:

Would I be able to obtain employment authorization while the investor petition is pending?

Answer:

No. You will not be able to apply for Green Card and employment authorization document until your petition is approved.

Question 177:

What is the minimum amount I have to invest in order to qualify as an immigrant investor?

Answer:

The minimum amount is subject to period change. However, currently it stands at $500,000 (Five Hundred Thousand Dollars) through a regional center; and $1,000,000 (One Million Dollars) through personal investment.

Question 178:

In meeting the requirement of creating minimum of 10 American jobs, can I buy an existing business as an immigrant investor?

Answer:

Yes. Employment creation may be direct job creation or indirect job creation by saving jobs that would have otherwise been lost.

Question 179:

Would I be able to obtain permanent residence through investment if I am already out of status in the United

States?

Answer:

No. Alien entrepreneurs are also required to meet all other eligibility requirements for Green Card, including being in legal status at the time of application.

Question 180:

Does my investment cover my spouse and children?

Answer:

Yes, it covers the investor, the spouse and children under 21 years old. It does not cover any child over 21 years at the time of filing.

Question 181:

What if my child is under 21 at the time of filing the investment petition but turned 21 while the processing is going on?

Answer:

Your child would still be protected under the Child Status Protection Act for as long as the petition has been received and acknowledged before your child's 21st birthday.

Question 182:

In applying for the investment petition, can I use a fund obtained as a loan?

Answer:

Yes, for as long as the collateral for the loan is

independent of the investment funds.

Question 183:

Can I use my spouse's income as part of the investment fund?

Answer:

Yes, you can use a combined income of a married couple.

Question 184:

Can the investment amount be a gift?

Answer:

Yes, it can be a gift. However, you will need to establish the kind of relationship that would warrant the gift of such an enormous amount of money. A parent or parents can give a child the investment amount on the basis of parental love and affection. A child can also give the parent the investment fund on the basis of family love and affection.

Question 185:

Upon the approval of my petition, and my application for permanent resident, would I get a 10-year Green Card?

Answer:

No. Upon the approval of your petition, and the approval of your application for permanent resident status, you will get a conditional Green Card.

Question 186:

Is it possible to obtain a 10-year Green Card directly if my application is based on investment?

Answer:

No. All applications for permanent resident based on investment is granted on conditional basis. In other words, no one can get a 10-year Green Card directly if the application is based on investment. The investor is granted a 2-year Green Card on the condition that the Green Card would only be extended upon satisfactory evidence that the funds were actually invested in line with the documentations provided at the initial filings.

This requirement is necessary and it is in the best interest of both parties because the investor may not be able to provide evidence that the investment actually created 10 American jobs at the initial stage. In fact, some investments may not have taken off at the time of the initial petition. On one hand, it would be unfair to the investor to require him/her to provide evidence of creation of 10 American jobs at the initial stage. On the other hand, USCIS would be able to verify employment creation before compensating the investor with a 10-year Green Card.

Question 187

If I file an immigrant petition for alien entrepreneur, would I still be able to obtain a visiting visa?

Answer:

Yes. You will still be able to come in and out of the United States. Usually an immigrant petition disqualifies someone from a non-immigrant visa, but in the case of an alien investor, it is understandable that someone who is able to afford the investment amount is not likely to overstay or become a public charge.

Over the years, I have been able to obtain F-1 status for a child of someone with a pending I-526 petition. Also, many of my clients with pending I-526 petitions have been able to renew their B1/B2 visas.

Question 188:

How long do I have to keep the fund invested?

Answer:

At the minimum, the investment fund must remain invested throughout the I-526 Petition process and for the first 2 years of the Green Card. However, if the investment were through a regional center, the terms of the subscription agreement would control the duration.

ADOPTION QUESTIONS

Question 189:
How can I adopt and bring my adopted child to the United States?

Answer:
There are 3 ways you can adopt and bring the adopted child to the United States. They are:

(1) As an orphan. You use Forms I-600A and I-600. (This option is available for children from a country that has not implemented The Hague Adoption Convention)

(2) Through The Hague Process. You use Forms I-800A and I-800. (This option is available for children from a country that has implemented The Hague Adoption Convention)

(3) Through the regular family based petition. You use Form I-130. (This option is available for children who does not meet the requirements of the first two options above).

Question 190:
What is Hague process?

Answer:
The Hague process is the procedure set up by The

Hague Convention on Protection of Children and Co-operation in Respect of Intercountry Adoption (Hague Adoption Convention). It is an international treaty that provides important safeguards to protect the best interests of children, birth parents, and adoptive parents who are involved in intercountry adoptions.

The Hague Adoption Convention entered into force in the United States on April 1, 2008. All cases filed on or after April 1, 2008, seeking to adopt a child from any country outside of the United States that is a party to the Convention must follow The Hague process.

Question 191:

What if I filed my Form I-600A, Application for Advance Processing of Orphan Petition or my Form I-600, Petition to Classify Orphan as an Immediate Relative before April 1, 2008?

Answer:

You may continue to process your case under the orphan regulations for as long as the prospective adoptive child's home country has not adopted The Hague Adoption Convention, or allows for continuation of processing for cases filed under prior laws.

Question 192:

What eligibility requirements do I have to meet in order to adopt a child from outside the United States?

Answer:

In order to adopt a child from outside the United States, you must meet the following requirements:

1. You must be a US citizen

2. You must be residing in the United States

3. If you are married, you and your spouse must sign the paperwork

4. If you are not married, you must be at least 24 years old when you commence the process

5. You must establish your ability to provide proper parental care by submitting a home study completed by an authorized adoption home study preparer.

Question 193:

How old does the prospective adopted child have to be to be eligible?

Answer:

The prospective adopted child must be under 16 years old at the time of filing Form I-800 if you are using The Hague process or under 16 at the time of adoption if you are using either the orphan process or the I-130 process.

Question 194:

If I am using the orphan process, is there an investigation before the case is approved?

Answer:

Yes. USCIS and/or Department of State does conduct investigation in the child's country to verify the following:

1. That the child is an orphan

2. That you have obtained a valid adoption or grant of custody.

3. That the child does not have an illness or disability that is not described in the orphan petition.

4. That the child does not have any special needs that were not fully addressed in your home study.

5. That the child qualifies for immigration as your adopted child.

Question 195:

If the child has medical problems, is there anything I can do?

Answer:

Yes, you may apply for waiver using Form I-601, Application for waiver of ground of inadmissibility.

Question 196:

Can I follow the orphan process despite the fact that my prospective adopted child is from a country that has signed The Hague Adoption Convention?

Answer:

No. If the child is from a country that has signed The Hague Adoption Convention, you will not be able to use the Orphan process. You must follow The Hague process.

Question 197:
Am I required to be familiar with the local laws of the prospective adopted child's country?

Answer:
It is not mandatory. However, it is better to be familiar with the local laws so that your efforts are not in vain. For example, in Lagos State Nigeria, Ministry of Social Welfare and the High Court Family Division in Lagos State, Nigeria notified the Department of State and the Department of Homeland Security that as of April 2016, Morgan Hill Children Foundation, a Nigerian non-profit organization that specializes in child welfare, must facilitate all intercountry adoptions from Lagos State, Nigeria.

Morgan Hill Children Foundation is presently the only organization authorized by Nigeria to facilitate inter-country adoptions from Lagos State of Nigeria. If you are not familiar with this information, and you adopt a child from Lagos State of Nigeria, your efforts may be fruitless.

In addition, if you are adopting from a Hague Convention country, and you are not familiar with the local laws, there may be restrictions that may prevent the adopted child from immigrating to the United States.

Question 198:
How can I find out if a particular country is Hague Convention country?

Answer:

To find out if a particular country has implemented The Hague Adoption Convention, you should check the Department of State website. The list is updated regularly. You may find information at: *https://travel.state.gov/content/adoptionsabroad/en/hague-convention/convention-countries.html*

Question 199:

What are the differences between Hague Process and Orphan process?

Answer:

There are several safeguards under The Hague process that are not available under the Orphan process. Some of them are as follows:

1. Under The Hague process, a country that is a party to the Convention must have an officially designated Central Authority to ensure that the adoption process is safeguarded.

The United States Central Authority is the Department of State. This means that all questions, and or clarifications about adoption in the United States must be directed to the Department of State by Hague Convention countries.

2. An Adoption Service Provider (ASP) must be accredited or otherwise authorized to provide adoption services in connection with a Hague adoption in order for the provider to assist the prospective adoptive parent(s) with a Hague adoption.

3. It is unlawful to adopt a child prior to filing Form I-800A and Form I-800 under The Hague Convention agreement.

4. Some Hague Convention countries requires post-adoption reporting on the progress and development of the child and how the child is adjusting to the new country. The requirements and frequency of these reports vary from country to country. Some countries permit adoptive families to prepare and submit the reports, while other countries expect a licensed social worker or the primary adoption service provider to prepare and submit the reports.

5. The Hague process requires minimum of 10 hours of parental education of the prospective adoptive parents.

6. The Hague process requires adoption records to be preserved for 75 years.

Question 200:

How do I know if an adoption service provider is accredited or authorized to provide adoption services?

Answer:

You have to check with the Central Authority. In addition, you should ask any adoption service provider whether the adoption service provider is authorized to work on Hague adoption cases before hiring or paying any money to the provider.

It is also important to note that an adoption service provider cannot provide legal advice or legal services to the prospective adoptive parent(s) or represent the prospective adoptive parent(s) before USCIS. Only Attorneys can give legal advice and represent the prospective adoptive parent(s) before USCIS. It is therefore important to ask a lot of questions and verify the answers before you make payment to any service provider.

Question 201:

What are the step by step procedure of The Hague Process?

Answer:

1. Select an accredited or authorized adoption service provider.

2. Select an Immigration Attorney.

3. Obtain a home study from someone authorized to complete Hague adoption home study.

4. File Form I-800A with USCIS in order to establish your eligibility and suitability.

5. Upon approval of Form I-800A, you should apply to the Central Authority of the other country for a specific adoption placement.

6. Once the Central Authority has proposed placing a child with you for adoption, but before you actually adopt the child, you must file Form I-800 on behalf of the child to be adopted to determine the child's eligibility to immigrate to the United

States based on the proposed adoption.

7. Wait for Form I-800 to be approved. You can either adopt the child in the other country or obtain custody of the child and bring the child to the United States to be adopted here.

8. Obtain an immigrant visa for the child. If you adopt your child in the other country, the child would obtain IH-3 immigrant visa, but if you obtain custody with the intention of completing the process here in the United States, the child would obtain IH-4 immigrant visa.

9. Bring the child to the United States with the visa.

10. Apply for citizenship for the child.

11. Ensure compliance with post adoption reporting if applicable to your specific case.

Question 202

What is post adoption reporting?

Answer:

Many countries require adoptive parents or adoption service providers to report on the child's progress and welfare after an adoption has concluded, sometimes for several years after the adoption took place.

Question 203:

What are the step by step procedure of the Orphan Process?

Answer:

1. Select an adoption service provider licensed in your state of residence.
2. Select an Immigration Attorney

3. Obtain a home study from someone that meets the requirements of your state of residence.

4. Unlike The Hague process, you may adopt or obtain legal custody of the child in the adoption country. (Please note that the local law of the country you are adopting a child from controls at this stage. Please find out the local laws and ensure compliance because the adoption would be investigated).

5. You may begin the orphan process before you identify a particular child for adoption by filing Form I-600A (Application of Advance Processing of Orphan Petition) Once a particular child has been identified, you would then file a Form I-600 (Petition to Classify Orphan as an Immediate Relative) for that child. You may also file both Form I-600 and Form I-600A simultaneously.

6. Upon approval, the National Visa Center will notify you by letter when your case has been assigned to a U.S. Embassy or Consulate abroad. The Embassy or Consulate will provide instructions on the next steps. A USCIS or consular officer in the child's country of residence then completes Form I-604 (Determination on Child for Adoption) to ensure the child has been properly classified as an orphan as defined by INA.

7. Submit immigrant visa application.

8. Bring the child to the United States.

Question 204:

How do you ensure that the child you want to adopt meets the definition of orphan as defined by Immigration and Nationality Act (INA)?

Answer:

You may seek advice from an experienced immigration Attorney before the adoption.

However, under the INA, an Orphan means that the child must have no parents, or a sole or surviving parent who is unable to care for the child and has, in writing, irrevocably released the child for adoption.

Question 205:

What are the step by step procedure of the regular family based I-130 petition?

Answer:

1. Identify and adopt a child in his or her home country. Ensure that all local adoption laws are followed.

2. The adoption must be full and final before the child turns 16 years old.

3. You must accrue two years of legal and physical custody of the child. Legal and physical custody can be accrued at one stretch of time or cumulatively over several periods. They can also be accrued before, during and after the adoption.

4. File Form I-130 Petition for Alien Relative for the child.

5. Upon approval of the petition, you continue the process with the National visa center.

6. Apply for immigrant visa at the US embassy.

7. Bring the child to the United States.

PART THREE

ASYLUM AND WITHHOLDING OF REMOVAL QUESTIONS

ASYLUM AND WITHHOLDING OF REMOVAL QUESTIONS

Question 206:

What is asylum?

Answer:

Asylum is a form of protection that allows individuals who are in the United States to remain here, provided that they meet the definition of refugee and are not barred from either applying for or being granted asylum, and eventually to adjust their status to lawful permanent resident.

Question 207:

Who is a refugee?

Answer:

Any person who is outside any country of such person's nationality or, in the case of a person having no nationality, is outside any country in which such person last habitually resided, and who is unable or unwilling to return to, and is unable or unwilling to avail himself or herself of the protection of that country because of persecution or a well-founded fear of persecution on account of race, religion, nationality, membership in a particular social group, or political opinion.

The term "refugee" does not include any person who ordered, incited, assisted, or otherwise participated in the persecution of any person on account of race, religion, nationality, membership in a particular social group, or political opinion.

Question 208:
What is the difference between asylum and refugee?

Answer:
They are basically the same except that you apply as a refugee when you are outside the United States and you apply for asylum when you are in the United States. Eligibility requirements and burden of proof are the same.

Question 209:
On what ground can I apply for asylum?

Answer:
You may apply for asylum on the basis of only one of the following:

1. Race

2. Nationality

3. Religion

4. Membership in a particular social group

5. Political opinion

Question 210:

Can I apply for asylum based on female genital mutilation?

Answer:

Yes. Female genital mutilation would fall under membership in a particular social group.

Question 211:

Can I apply for asylum based on gang violence in my country?

Answer:

No. Gang violence is not recognized as a particular social group. However, you may need to consult an experienced immigration Attorney to evaluate your specific situation and advise you accordingly.

Question 212:

Can someone who has been forced to abort a pregnancy qualify for asylum?

Answer:

A person who has been forced to abort a pregnancy or to undergo involuntary sterilization, or who has been persecuted for failure or refusal to undergo such a procedure or for other resistance to a coercive population control program, shall be deemed to have been persecuted on account of political opinion, and a person who has a well-founded fear that he or she will be forced to undergo such a procedure or subject to persecution for such failure, refusal, or resistance shall be deemed to have a well-founded fear of persecution on account of political opinion.

Question 213:
I have been living in the United States for two years. I want to apply for asylum. What are my chances?

Answer:
You may not qualify for asylum because you are outside the one-year window. However, it is better to consult an experienced immigration Attorney to look into your peculiar situation and advise you accordingly.

Question 214:
My asylum application was denied and I was ordered removed from the United States. I appealed the decision to the Board of Immigration Appeals but I am now married to a US citizen. How can I fix my status?

Answer:
Your spouse should file a relative petition on your behalf. Upon the approval of the petition, you may file a motion to re-open your case with the Board of Immigration Appeals for an opportunity to apply for adjustment of status. Your motion should explain that the relief of adjustment of status was not available at the initial trial.

Question 215:
My asylum application has been pending for more than one year. I have not been invited for interview. Is it possible to get my case expedited?

Answer:

Yes. You may get your case expedited by writing a letter to the asylum office where your application is pending to request expedited processing. Upon the receipt of your letter, the asylum office will add your name to what is called the short list.

Your letter should state clearly that you are willing to attend interview at very short notice.

Please be sure that you have all your supporting documents ready before you take this step. This is because applicant on short list are usually invited for interview when someone who was previously scheduled for interview cancelled the appointment or request a rescheduling of the appointment.

The notice may be so short that you may not even receive a letter in the mail. You may receive a phone call requesting you to come for interview the following day or in 2 days' time. If your documentations are not ready, and you requested to be placed on short list, it may lead to the denial of your application.

Question 216:

I entered the United States without inspection (EWI) through a land border with Mexico. I declared my intention to apply for asylum. I was given credible fear interview. A notice to Appear was issued to enable me present my asylum application before an immigration judge. I was then paroled into the United States to enable me attend my immigration court proceedings. Can I get a work authorization while waiting for my hearing at the immigration court?

Answer:

Yes. You may be able to apply for employment authorization document to enable you work. However, employment authorization would only be given to you to expire on the expiration of the parole.

You may also be eligible to apply for employment authorization based on your pending asylum application if the application has been pending for at least 150 days.

Question 217:

I was granted parole and I used it to apply for employment authorization. My employment authorization document expired the same date my parole expired. How can I renew my employment authorization?

Answer:

Usually employment authorization is granted to expire on the expiration of parole. What you can do is to request an extension of your parole. If you are waiting for a hearing in immigration court proceedings, you should apply for an extension of your parole with the Customs and Border Protection (CBP) using your immigration court hearing notice. Your parole may be extended until your hearing date and you may then use the extension to apply for a renewal of your employment authorization document.

Question 218:

I entered the United States without a visa. I declared my intention to apply for asylum and I was given a credible fear interview. I was subsequently paroled. Can I change my status?

Answer:

No. You may not change your status on these facts. In order to be eligible for change of status in the United States, you will need to provide evidence of legal entry. Parole for asylum purpose would not satisfy this requirement.

Question 219:

I entered the United States without a visa. I declared my intention to apply for asylum and I was given a credible fear interview. I was subsequently paroled. My asylum application is still pending. I am now married to a United States citizen. Can I adjust my status?

Answer:

Yes. You may be able to adjust your status if your United States citizen spouse filed I-130 petition on your behalf and the petition is approved. However, only USCIS has jurisdiction over your case. You may not adjust at the immigration court. See 8 C.F.R. §245.2(a)(1).

Question 220:

I was granted withholding of removal by the immigration judge. How can I obtain employment authorization Document?

Answer:

You should apply for employment authorization with USCIS attaching a copy of the immigration judge's order granting you withholding of removal to your application.

Question 221:

I applied for asylum and withholding of removal at the immigration court. The judge denied my asylum application but granted my withholding application. I am now married to a United States citizen. How can I get Green Card?

Answer:

USCIS does not have jurisdiction over your adjustment application. Your United States citizen spouse may file I-130 petition on your behalf. Upon approval, you will need to file a motion to re-open your removal proceedings with the same immigration court that granted you withholding of removal. You have a choice of either requesting the immigration court to set a trial date for your adjustment application or request the court to terminate the proceedings to enable USCIS have jurisdiction to adjudicate your adjustment application.

PART FOUR

CITIZENSHIP QUESTIONS

CITIZENSHIP QUESTIONS

Question 222:

How can someone acquire United States citizenship?

Answer:

Citizenship can be acquired by one of 4 (four) ways:

1. By Birth in the United States

2. By Birth outside the United States if at least one parent is a United States citizen. The US citizen parent must have resided in the United States for at least 5 (five) years before the child was born. Period of legal permanent residency will count towards the 5 (five) year requirement. The birth of the child must be reported to the US consulate in the country where the child is born at the earliest opportunity possible.

3. Parental citizenship of children under 18 years old where the child is a legal permanent resident and is residing in the legal and physical custody of the citizen parent in the United States.

4. By Naturalization

Question 223:

I am a naturalized US citizen in the US military and I am stationed in South Korea. I have a 16-year-old son.

My son is not a permanent resident and he does not reside in the United States, how can I obtain citizenship for him under parental citizenship category?

Answer:

The requirements of being a legal permanent resident and physical residence are waived for members of the Armed Forces residing abroad for as long as the child is under 18 years old and not married.

Question 224:

What are the requirements of naturalization?

Answer:

Depending on the category under which you are applying, the basic requirements are:

• An applicant is not required to be a Legal Permanent Resident (Green Card holder) if he/she is a United States National. (A non-citizen who owes permanent allegiance to the United States that means persons born in or having ties with an outlying possession of the United States. Example is Guam, Puerto Rico, U.S. Virgin Islands, American Samoa, Swains Island and the Commonwealth of the Northern Mariana Islands (CNMI).

• Must be a Green Card holder for 5 (five) years or

•Must be a Green Card holder for 3 (three) years if married to a US citizen or

• Must be a Green Card holder for 1 (one) day if you are

in active military service or

• Must be a Green Card holder for 1 (one) day if you are married to a US citizen who died during honorable active duty service in the US Armed Forces. (Must be married to, and living with the US citizen spouse at the time of death) or

• Must be a Green Card holder for 1 (one) day if you are the spouse of a US citizen who is a member of the US Armed Forces or

• Must be a Green Card holder for 1 (one) day if you are an employee or an individual under contract to the US Government or

• Must be a Green Card holder for 1 (one) day if you are an employee of an American Research Institution recognized by the Attorney General of the United States or

• Must be a Green Card holder for 1 (one) day if you are an employee of an American owned firm or corporation engaged in the foreign trade and commerce for the United States or

• Must be a Green Card holder for 1 (one) day if you are an employee of a public international organization of which the United States is a member by law or treaty (e.g. United Nations) or

• Must be a Green Card holder for 1 (one) day if you are a person who performs ministerial or priestly functions for a religious denomination or an interdenominational organization with a valid presence in the United States AND you will be proceeding to join your spouse whose work abroad under orders of the qualifying employer will continue for at least 1 (one) year after the date you will be naturalized.

In addition, an applicant must meet these other requirements:

- Must be a person of good moral character for 5 (five) years from the date of Green Card or 3 (three) years in the case of someone who is married to a United States citizen.

- Must be attached to the Principles of the constitution and well disposed to the good order and happiness of the United States.

- Must be able to read and write and demonstrate the knowledge of English, US History and government or be exempt from any of them.

- If the applicant is a male between ages 18 and 26, the applicant must register with selective service and must not receive relief from selective service based on alienage.

- Must not be in removal proceedings.

- Must not be a deserter during war time

- Must not be a member of communist party.

- Must be willing to bear arms on behalf of the United States.

- Must be willing to perform noncombatant service or work of national importance.

Question 225:
What constitutes bad moral character or lack of good moral character?

Answer:
The following are examples of what constitutes lack of good moral character.

- Falsely claiming to be a US citizen (there is no waiver for it)

- Voting unlawfully

- Giving false testimony

- Outstanding child support (nonsupport of your dependents)

- Adultery tending to destroy a marriage (especially when you obtained your Green Card through the marriage)

- Commission of criminal acts

- Failure to pay fines for traffic violations

- Failure to pay back Taxes to IRS

- Habitual drunkenness

Question 226:

What is the difference between a US citizen and a US national?

Answer:

The only difference is that US nationals cannot vote or hold elected office. Otherwise, both are eligible to apply for US passport and the passports are exactly the same. Both passports usually list USA as the nationality. Both can reside and work anywhere in the United States without restriction.

Question 227:

How can a US national acquire the right to vote or hold elected office?

Answer:

US nationals are eligible to apply for US citizenship. They have to meet the same eligibility requirements as Green Card holders except the requirement of first being a legal permanent resident.

Question 228:

How long do I have to wait to apply for Citizenship by naturalization?

Answer:

It depends on a lot of factors. It ranges from 1 day to 5 years. If you or your spouse is in active military duty, you may be eligible to apply 1 day after becoming a permanent resident. If you have been married to a US citizen for 3 years after becoming a permanent resident, you will be eligible to apply. Other eligibility requires that you must have been a permanent resident for 5 years. Please note that there are other eligibility requirements.

Question 229:

I am a Green card holder. My children also have Green Card. If I become a US citizen, does it cover my children?

Answer:

If you and your children are Green Card holders and you subsequently become a US citizen, all your children who are Green Card holders and are under 18 years old on the day you become a US citizen would automatically become US citizen but any of your children over 18 years old would need to apply for naturalization separately.

Question 230:

If my children become US citizen automatically when I naturalized, how do I obtain proof of citizenship for them?

Answer:

You can apply for US passport for them and use that as evidence of their citizenship. However, if you want citizenship certificate for them, you may apply for a certificate by filing Form N-600 with USCIS.

Question 231:

Can a US citizen be deported?

Answer:
No. A US citizen may not be deported or removed from the United States.

Question 232:
Can citizenship be revoked based on commission of a crime?

Answer:
No. US citizenship may not be revoked based on commission of a crime. If a US citizen committed a crime, he/she would face the consequence as prescribed by the law.

Question 233:
Under what circumstances can a US citizenship be revoked?

Answer:
US citizenship may be revoked if the citizenship was obtained by fraud in the first place. You cannot build something on nothing. However, once a US citizenship has been granted, whether it was obtained by fraud or not, only the court can revoke it after trial and conviction. Upon revocation, the person is then placed in removal proceedings.

Question 234:
I am a US citizen. My child who is 14 years old committed a crime, will my child lose his citizenship?

Answer:
No. He may be punished for his crime but he cannot lose his citizenship on the basis of his crime.

Question 235:
How many days is a permanent resident required to be physically present in the United States in order to be eligible for citizenship?

Answer:
It depends on the eligibility category. If you are required to be a permanent resident for 3 or 5 years before you are eligible, you will be required to be physically present in the United States for 50% of the time.

Question 236:
My parent is a permanent resident but she cannot read or write, how can he/she become a US citizen?

Answer:
There are few exceptions to the reading, writing, and knowledge of civics requirements of US citizenship. They are:

1. Applicants who are over 50 years old and have lived in the United States for 20 (twenty) years in Lawful Permanent Resident status. English would be exempted for this class of applicants but they would still have to take the civics test in the language of their choice.

2. Applicants who are over 55 years old and have lived in the United States for 15 (fifteen) years in Lawful

Permanent Resident status. English would be exempted for this class of applicants but they would still have to take the civics test in the language of their choice
3. Applicants who are over 65 years old and have lived in the United States for 20 years in Lawful Permanent Resident status. English would be exempted for this class of applicants but they would still have to take a simpler version of the civics test in the language of their choice. They would be tested on 10 (ten) out of 25 (twenty-five) simpler version of civics test in any language of their choice. They are required to answer 6 (six) questions correctly.

*Please note that applicants must still meet other eligibility requirements like good moral character.

Question 237:

Is there a medical disability exception for becoming a US citizen?

Answer:

Yes. Applicants who are physically or developmentally disabled or applicants who have mental impairments would be exempt from the requirements of reading, writing, and civics. A Medical Doctor, Osteopath, or Clinical Psychologist who are experienced in diagnosing the ailments would have to complete Form N-648 (Medical certifications for Disability Exceptions). This N-648 must be filed along with Form N-400 (Application for Naturalization).

*Please note that applicants must still meet other

eligibility requirements like good moral character.

Question 238:

As a US citizen, who can I file a petition for besides my parents?

Answer:

A US citizen may file a relative petition on behalf of family members. Under the immigration laws, family members include your father, mother, your spouse, and your children under 21 years old. In addition, you may file a petition on behalf of your siblings and your stepchild provided the marriage that created the step relationship occurred before the child's 18th birthday.

PART FIVE

IMMIGRATION AND CRIME QUESTIONS

IMMIGRATION AND CRIME QUESTIONS

Question 239:
Can a Legal Permanent Resident be deported based on crime?

Answer:
Yes. A legal permanent resident who committed a crime or multiple crimes may be removed from the United States upon final conviction.

Question 240:
I am a legal permanent resident. I was arrested and charged for family violence, a felony, but my case is still pending. Am I removable from the United States?

Answer:
You will have to wait until the criminal case is over before you determine your faith. If the case is dismissed or there is no conviction, you may escape the consequence of the crime. In addition, depending on the conviction, you may be eligible for some limited waiver like re-adjustment and 212(c) waivers or EOIR 42A Cancellation of removal for legal permanent residence.

Question 241:
What constitute a final conviction of a crime for

immigration purpose?

Answer:

Under 8 U.S.C. 1101(A)(48), a conviction is final if these elements are met:

1. The alien has pled guilty or no contest, or the alien has admitted facts sufficient to support a conclusion or finding of guilt, or has been found guilty by a judge or jury and

2. The alien is adjudged guilty, or where adjudication is withheld, the court has imposed some form of restriction on the alien's liberty. Examples are going to prison; reporting to a probation officer; paying fine; or refraining from some form of activity.

Question 242:

I am charged with a crime. My criminal defense Attorney negotiated a non-incarceration suspension for me. Would that constitute a conviction for immigration purpose?

Answer:

No. Non-incarceration suspension does not constitute a conviction.

Question 243:

Is a case taken under advisement a conviction for immigration purpose?

Answer:

A case taken under advisement is not a conviction for immigration purpose as the judge has not made any final disposition to remove the case from calendar. See Pino v. Landon, 349 U.S. 901 (1955) ("On file" status meaning the case remains on the records of the court but no further action is normally taken, does not constitute a final conviction).

Question 244:

Is a deferred sentence a conviction for immigration purpose?

Answer:

A deferred sentence or a sentence with suspended imposition is a final conviction for immigration purpose. This is because a sentence remains a sentence for immigration purposes, even if imposition or execution of the sentence has been suspended. See 8 U.S.C. 1101(a)(48)(B).

Question 245:

Is a pre-prosecution probation (like the one you enter into for speeding ticket) or pre-trial diversion a final conviction?

Answer:

No. Pre-prosecution probation or pre-trial diversion is not a final conviction (AILA InfoNet Doc. No. 09011560). However, I would caution that it depends on whether an admission of guilt is part of entry into the program. Programs that require an admission of guilt and then some period of court-ordered probation or community service, followed by setting aside of the conviction on successful completion of that program, do constitute convictions for immigration purposes.

Question 246:

Is deferral of prosecution a conviction for immigration purpose?

Answer:

A deferral of prosecution or a general continuance to monitor the alien for good behavior without entering a plea or admitting the charges, followed by a dismissal, is not a conviction.

Question 247:

Is a case on appeal a conviction for immigration purpose?

Answer:

No. A case on direct appeal is not a final conviction. See Matter of Thomas 21 I&N Dec. 20 (BIA 1995).

Question 248:

Is payment of restitution a conviction for immigration purpose?

Answer:

Payment of restitution in lieu of prosecution is not a conviction for immigration purpose.

Question 249:
Is dismissal a conviction for immigration purpose?

Answer:
Dismissal and finding of not guilty is not a conviction for immigration purpose.

Question 250:
I was convicted of two counts but it was a single misconduct. Does the fact that it was a single misconduct affect the consequence for immigration purpose?

Answer:
Where two crimes arose out of a single criminal misconduct, it would be considered a single scheme of criminal misconduct for immigration purpose.

Question 251:
I was convicted of simple possession of controlled substance. My conviction has been expunged. Would that affect my immigration status?

Answer:
No. 18 USC § 3607(a) provides that an expungement of a first simple possession plea eliminates the conviction for all legal purposes. However, Section 3607(a) also provides that a violation of probation will bar this relief.

Question 252:
Is it every conviction that disqualify a non-citizen from obtaining immigration benefit or relief?

Answer:

No. It is not every conviction that disqualify a non-citizen from benefit or relief. However, where the conviction is for an aggravated felony offense, it may disqualify an alien from obtaining any immigration benefit, or any form of relief except there is a viable defense.

Question 253:

I am in removal proceeding and charged with being convicted of aggravated felony but conviction documents clearly show that I was convicted of misdemeanor at the state court. How can I fix this?

Answer:

A misdemeanor under state law may be categorized as a felony or aggravated felony under immigration law. For immigration purpose, crimes are categorized by the type of conduct involved rather than distinguished between felony and misdemeanor. The nature of offense, the type of conviction, and the maximum potential penalty are factors that are considered for immigration purpose.

Usually a sentence of less than one year may save a non-citizen from immigration consequences.

Question 254:

What constitute aggravated felony under immigration law?

Answer:

The nature of a crime and the sentence imposed determines the classification for immigration purpose.

Here is a list of aggravated felony offenses for immigration purpose.

1. Murder

2. Rape

3. Sexual abuse of a minor

4. Drug-trafficking crimes or any illicit trafficking in any controlled substances.

5. Illicit trafficking in destructive devices.

6. Many firearms offenses, though a simple possession of an unlicensed firearm by a permanent resident is often not an aggravated felony.

7. Any offense related to laundering of monetary instruments if the amount exceeds $10,000.

8. Most offenses involving explosives or arson.

9. Offenses relating to the receipt, manufacture, or possession of firearms without proper licenses or taxes.

10. Most crimes of violence (not including a purely political offense) for which the term of imprisonment imposed (regardless of any suspension of such imprisonment) is at least one year.

11. A Theft offense (including receipt of stolen property) or burglary offense for which the term of imprisonment

imposed (regardless of any suspension of such imprisonment) is at least one year.

12. Ransom offenses, including using interstate communications to demand ransom or threaten kidnap; using mails to make threatening communications; making threatening communications from foreign countries; receiving, possessing, or disposing of ransom money or property.

13. Child pornography offenses, including employing, using, or coercing minors to engage in pornography; selling or transferring custody of a child with knowledge that the child will be used for pornography; receiving or distributing child pornography.

14. RICO (the Racketeer-Influenced and Corrupt Organizations Act) offenses for which a sentence of one year imprisonment or more may be imposed.

15. Offenses relating to owning, controlling, managing, or supervising a prostitution business.

16. Offenses relating to involuntary servitude.

17. Offenses relating to spying and national security.

18. Treason and concealing and failing to disclose treason.

19. Fraud or deceit crimes in which the loss to the victim exceeds $10,000.

20. Income tax evasion where the loss to the government exceeds $10,000.

21. Alien smuggling for commercial gain where the term of imprisonment imposed (regardless of any suspension of imprisonment) is at least one year (exception: only one offense where the person smuggled was your spouse, parent, or child).

22. Document fraud under which the person's actions constitute trafficking in the documents and the sentence imposed (even if suspended) is at least one year (except where you committed the offense to assist your spouse, parent, or child).

23. An offense for failing to appear for sentence where a defendant has been convicted of a crime with a possible sentence of 15 years or more.

24. Offenses involving obstruction of justice, perjury, or subornation or helping another person commit perjury or bribery of a witness, for which a sentence of a least one year may be imposed.

25. Offenses relating to commercial bribery, forgery, counterfeiting, or trafficking in vehicles, for which a sentence of at least one year may be imposed.

26. Offenses committed by an alien ordered previously deported.

27. Offenses relating to the failure to appear in court for a criminal offense for which a sentence of two or more

years may be imposed.

28. Any attempt or conspiracy to commit any of the above acts, committed within the United States.

29. Any attempt or conspiracy to commit any of these acts violating a law in a foreign country where the term of imprisonment was completed within the previous 15 years.

PART SIX

IMMIGRATION COURT QUESTIONS

IMMIGRATION COURT QUESTIONS

Question 255:

I have been placed in a removal proceeding. My friends advised me not to go because I could be arrested. Should I go?

Answer:

Yes, you should go. Removal proceeding is a place where you will have the opportunity to present a relief to the immigration judge. It is a place where you will have the opportunity to tell the immigration judge why you believe you should stay in the United States. It is a place where an application that has been denied by USCIS may be reviewed. It is a place where the immigration judge may be able to do what USCIS is not capable of doing. (You may be able to get Green Card through Cancellation of removal despite not entering the United States with a visa. USCIS cannot grant Cancellation of removal).

Not going will deprive you of this benefit. It would also add to your immigration problems because the fact that you did not show up will not stop the immigration judge from ordering you removed in absentia.

Question 256:

I applied for asylum and it was denied. I am now in removal proceedings. What can I do?

Answer:

When an asylum officer does not approve your asylum application, you would be issued a referral notice. This notice is not a denial of your asylum application. You will have an opportunity to represent your application before an immigration judge in removal proceedings.

Question 257:

I have been living in the United States for 12 years. My spouse is a United States citizen. I have two United States citizen children. ICE recently arrested me. What are my chances of not being deported?

Answer:

Based on these facts, you may be eligible for Cancellation of removal for non-permanent resident. You should contact an experienced immigration Attorney.

Question 258:

I am in removal proceedings in New York. I now live in Dallas. Can I transfer my case to Dallas?

Answer:

Yes. You have to file a motion to change venue.

Question 259:

I am in a removal proceeding. Can I obtain an employment authorization document?

Answer:

It depends on your peculiar situation and what relief

you are entitled to. Generally, applicants seeking adjustment and Cancellation of removal may be able to obtain or renew employment authorization document. For those seeking asylum or withholding of removal, they may be able to apply for employment authorization after their case has been pending for at least 150 days.

Question 260:

What could lead to someone being placed in removal/ deportation proceedings?

Answer:

Several things can bring an illegal alien to the attention of the authorities. Some of them include:

1. Asylum application that is not granted by an immigration officer.

2. Adjustment application denied by USCIS

3. Petition to remove condition on permanent resident denied by USCIS.

4. Permanent resident who committed a crime.

5. Alien arrested by Immigration and Customs Enforcement for visa overstay.

6. Undocumented alien arrested by ICE

7. Arriving alien not in possession of immigrant visa.

8. Arrest by local police where ICE detainer is enforced.

Question 261:

I am in removal proceedings; the judge said that I should have received an NTA, what is an NTA?

Answer:

NTA means Notice to Appear. It is document notifying the alien to appear in court to answer to the allegations contained therein. Usually it contains the reasons why ICE believes that the alien should be removed from the United States

Question 262:

An immigration judge previously ordered me removed from the United States but I was not aware of the order because I was not in court. Therefore I did not leave. I am now married to a US citizen and we have two children. How can I get a Green Card?

Answer:

For as long as the removal order is there, you cannot get Green Card. Your US citizen spouse should file Form I-130 Petition for Alien Relative on your behalf. Upon approval, you should then file a motion to re-open with the same immigration court that ordered you removed.

It is better to contact an experienced immigration Attorney to help you navigate the process because you stand the risk of being arrested during your I-130 interview.

Question 263:

I was ordered removed in Michigan but I did not leave.

I relocated to Texas. I am now married to a US citizen. How can I fix my status?

Answer:

Relocating to a different state does not solve your problem. The removal order is enforceable all over the country. You will need to contact an experienced immigration Attorney to look into your peculiar situation and advise you appropriately.

Question 264:

I was ordered removed by an immigration judge. I was immediately arrested and detained by Immigration and Customs Enforcement (ICE) agents. I filed an appeal with the Board of Immigration Appeals (BIA). I was detained for six months before my Attorney was able to get me out. Upon my release from detention, I decided to move back to Mexico. Two weeks after I got to Mexico, the BIA remanded my case to the immigration judge with instruction to review and approve my case. How can I come back to the US and get my Green Card?

Answer:

What you did is known as self-deportation. Because you left the United States on your own before your appeal was adjudicated, you abandon any form of relief you may be entitled to.

Question 265:

I am in a removal proceeding. One of the allegation in my Notice to Appear is that I falsely claim to be a US citizen on my I-9 Employment Eligibility Verification. Can I apply for a waiver?

Answer:

There is no waiver for falsely claiming to be a US citizen. However, I will suggest that you consult with an experienced immigration Attorney to look into your case and determine if there are other relief you may be eligible for.

Question 266:

I was placed in a removal proceeding about twenty years ago. I was advised at the time not to go to court because I could be arrested. I did not attend the proceedings. My son is now over 21 years old and he wants to petition for me. How can I go about it?

Answer:

The best thing to do under these circumstances is to contact an experienced immigration Attorney to help you look into your peculiar case. There are many questions that requires answer before you can get a proper advise. How did you get into removal proceeding in the first place? Were you ordered removed in absentia? An experienced immigration Attorney will be able to help you.

PART SEVEN

FEDERAL DISTRICT COURT IMMIGRATION QUESTIONS

FEDERAL DISTRICT COURT IMMIGRATION QUESTIONS

Question 267:

I applied for Citizenship. I completed my biometrics and I have been interviewed. However, it has been more than one year since my interview and I am yet to receive a decision on my application. What can I do?

Answer:

Immigration law is not a one cap fits all. For that reason, I will suggest that you consult an experienced immigration Attorney. However, assuming there are no other complex issues of eligibility, you should file a Mandamus action at the federal District court against USCIS.

Mandamus is an action requesting the federal district court to mandate USCIS to adjudicate the case in line with the regulations. Mandamus should be the last resort. It should only be filed after every other legitimate step has been taken without headway.

The regulation generally provides that citizenship application should be adjudicated within ninety (90) days after interview. It is pertinent to point out the fact that in these days of terrorism, and the need for proper screening of applicants, the 90 days may not be feasible in some cases.

However, a mandamus action will compel USCIS to either adjudicate or provide a legitimate explanation of why the case is delayed. In my over a dozen year of filing Mandamus action, I have not experienced a single case of acceptable legitimate reason for delay accepted by District courts.

Question 268:

Will a mandamus action force USCIS to approve my case?

Answer:

No. Mandamus does not force USCIS to approve a case. What it does is to force USCIS to adjudicate a case. Mandamus will not make USCIS approve an unapprovable case. Similarly, it will not make USCIS deny an approvable case.

Question 269:

Will there be a backlash for filing Mandamus against USCIS?

Answer:

No. That will be in violation of the law. However, if you don't have a strong case, it is advisable not to file Mandamus. It should only be filed when there is no option.

Question 270:

Is Mandamus available for citizenship cases only?

Answer:

No. It is available for citizenship and all other immigration actions including family and employment based petitions or applications.

Question 271:

I applied for naturalization. USCIS denied my application on the ground of lack of good moral character. I filed Form N-336, request for a Hearing on a Decision in Naturalization Proceedings and it was also denied. What else can I do?

Answer:

You can apply to the District Court to have the court review the decision by USCIS.

Question 272:

I applied for adjustment of status based on an immigrant petition filed on my behalf by my US citizen spouse and both the petition and my adjustment application were denied. Can I file an action at the District court for review?

Answer:

No. District court is not the right place to file an appeal. Besides, as a foreign national, you do not have a right of appeal over the case. However, your US citizen spouse may file an appeal with the Board of Immigration Appeals ("The BIA" or "The Board") only your spouse may sign the appeal. If you sign the appeal The Board would not have jurisdiction over your case.

Question 273:
What can we do if the BIA denied our appeal?

Answer:
You can file an appeal with the Circuit Court with jurisdiction over your residence.

Question 274:
I applied for adjustment of status based on an immigrant petition filed on my behalf by employer and both the petition and my adjustment application was denied. Can I file an action at the District court for review?

Answer:
No. District court is not the right place to file an appeal. Besides, as a foreign national, you do not have a right of appeal over the case. However, your employer may file an appeal with the Administrative Appeals Office ("AAO") only your employer may sign the appeal. If you sign the appeal The AAO would not have jurisdiction over your case.

Question 275:
What can we do if the AAO denied our appeal?

Answer:
You may request a review of the AAO decision with the District Court with jurisdiction over your case.

PART EIGHT

WAIVER QUESTIONS

NON-IMMIGRANT VISA WAIVER QUESTIONS

Question 276:

I applied for a visiting visa but was denied because I was previously found inadmissible and denied entry at the point of entry. Is there a waiver I can file?

Answer:

Yes. You can apply for a 212(d)(3) waiver, which waives most grounds of inadmissibility including unlawful presence, criminal convictions, health issues, and other immigration violations. It is usually issued for either 6 (six) months or 1 (one) year but it may only be issued for a maximum of 5 (five) years.

Question 277:

Where is the non-immigrant visa waiver application filed?

Answer:

It should be filed at the US embassy in your home country. However, final decision is made by the Admissibility Review Office in Washington DC.

Question 278:

What is the procedure for filing the non-immigrant visa waiver?

Answer:

Generally, the applicant should complete Form I-192 except your specific consulate does not require it. Please find out from your consulate if you need to use the form. Include the filing fee, provide a detailed statement addressing the requirements, complete and attach a non-immigrant visa application to the US embassy for processing. The consular officer will review your form and make recommendation to the Admissibility Review Office in Washington DC for a final decision.

Question 279:

What are the requirements of non-immigrant visa waiver?

Answer:

An applicant for a non-immigrant visa waiver must provide a detailed statement where the following must positively be addressed.

1. Purpose in seeking to enter the United States and how important the purpose is.

2. The seriousness of the acts or omission which caused you to be inadmissible.

3. The risks in admitting you to the United States.

Question 280:

Can the non-immigrant visa waiver waive all grounds of inadmissibility?

Answer:

No. It cannot waive some criminal grounds, including sabotage, genocide, and espionage.

IMMIGRANT VISA WAIVER QUESTIONS

Question 281:

I falsely claimed to be a US citizen for the purpose of employment on Form I-9, Employment Eligibility Verification. Is there a waiver for that?

Answer:

No. There is no waiver for False Claim to US citizenship.

Question 282:

My previous spouse filed a petition on my behalf. It was denied because of marriage fraud. Is there a waiver I can file?

Answer:

No. Once a determination of marriage fraud has been made by USCIS, and the BIA did not reverse it on appeal, no other petition can be approved and there is no waiver for the marriage fraud.

Question 283:

While I was a permanent resident, my wife applied for a visiting visa and was denied. Out of desperation to join me, she obtained a new passport in a different name and applied again. She was denied again. I am now a US citizen. Is there a waiver for her actions and if yes what is the procedure?

Answer:

Yes. Your wife may be eligible for misrepresentation waiver. You will have to file a petition on behalf of your wife. Upon approval of the petition, you should pursue consular processing. Your wife would be denied at the embassy. You may then apply for a misrepresentation waiver.

Question 284:

Can I apply for a misrepresentation waiver as soon as my petition is approved?

Answer:

No. Your immigrant visa application would have to be denied at the embassy before you can apply for a waiver.

Question 285:

Under what circumstances can I apply for a waiver before going to the US embassy for an immigrant visa interview?

Answer:

Only if you are physically and unlawfully present in the United States and you are required to apply for provisional unlawful presence waiver. In this case, you may file your waiver application as soon as your I-130 Petition for alien relative is approved and before you leave the United States.

Question 286:

I am married to a US citizen. When a petition was filed on my behalf, my husband did not list my children because they are not here in the US. I am now a conditional permanent resident. How can I bring my children?

Answer:

This simply means that you obtain your conditional permanent resident status by misrepresentation when you did not disclose that you have children. Both the Form I-130 Petition for Alien Relative and Form I-485 Application to Register Permanent Resident or Adjust Status require you to list all your children. It is not a condition to the required disclosure that your children be present in the United States.

Failure to disclose the information constitutes a fraud that cut off USCIS line of inquiry to your background or even to the good faith requirement of your marriage. For that reason, you may lose your conditional permanent resident status.

You may apply for fraud or misrepresentation waiver. You should then disclose all the information and set the record straight. Your US citizen spouse should be your qualifying relative for the waiver. However, it is advisable that you consult with an experienced immigration Attorney to handle this very delicate process on your behalf.

Question 287:

What evidence do I need to provide in order to get my

waiver approved?

Answer:

Every case is different. It is better to consult an experienced Immigration Attorney for your specific case. However, generally, when you are applying for a waiver of a ground of inadmissibility based on extreme hardship to a qualifying relative, you have to provide the following:

1. Completed Form I-601

2. Very detailed letter of hardship from all qualifying relatives explaining the hardship the qualifying relative will encounter if the waiver is denied.

3. Evidence of citizenship of all qualifying relatives in the form of Birth Certificates or Certificate of Naturalization.

4. Evidence of Legal Permanent Residence of all qualifying relatives (if applicable).

5. Evidence of medical problems (if applicable).

6. Evidence of qualifying relative's financial problem (if applicable).

7. Evidence of psychological problem. Example: evidence of treatment for depression, etc. (if applicable).

8. Evidence of country condition (if relying on country condition).

9. U.S. Department of State country report on your country (if relying on major political problem in your country).

10. Evidence of beneficiary's financial support of the qualifying relative.

11. Evidence of beneficiary's other forms of support of the qualifying relative.

12. Notarized letter from family members who have knowledge of the hardship the qualifying relative will suffer.

13. Notarized letters from friends who have knowledge of the hardship.

14. Support letters from prominent members of the society (example Congressman, Community Leaders, religious leaders, etc.)

15. Evidence of any form of recognition or award in the community.

16. Breakdown of monthly income and expenses of the household.

17. Any other document you have that may be specific to your case.

Question 288:

I am a Canadian citizen. I previously came to the United States under the visa waiver program. I stayed beyond

90 days and I have now been found to be inadmissible. Is there a waiver I can file?

Answer:

Yes. You may apply for non-immigrant waiver by using Form I-192, Application for Advance Permission to Enter as a non-immigrant. The Form should be submitted to Customs and Border Protection (CBP) officers at a US port of entry.

Please note that not all US embassies use Form I-192. It is better to find out from your specific embassy or CBP in the case of Canada if you need to use Form I-192.

Made in the USA
Monee, IL
04 November 2026

67383030R10105